The Religious Test

ALSO BY DAMON LINKER

The Theocons: Secular America Under Siege

The Religious Test

Why We Must Question
the Beliefs of Our Leaders

Damon Linker

W. W. NORTON & COMPANY

NEW YORK LONDON

Excerpts from "Aubade" and "Faith Healing" from
Collected Poems by Philip Larkin, Faber and Faber Ltd.
Excerpts from "Aubade" and "Faith Healing" from *Collected Poems* by Philip Larkin.
Copyright © 1988, 2003 by the Estate of Philip Larkin. Reprinted by
permission of Farrar, Straus and Giroux, LLC.

For information about permission to reproduce selections from this book,
write to Permissions, W. W. Norton & Company, Inc.,
500 Fifth Avenue, New York, NY 10110

For information about special discounts for bulk purchases, please contact
W. W. Norton Special Sales at specialsales@wwnorton.com or 800-233-4830

Manufacturing by Courier Westford
Book design by Chris Welch Design
Production manager: Julia Druskin

Library of Congress Cataloging-in-Publication Data

Linker, Damon, 1969–
The religious test : why we must question the beliefs of our leaders / Damon Linker.—1st ed.
p. cm.
Includes bibliographical references and index.
ISBN 978-0-393-06795-8 (hardcover)
1. Religion and politics—United States. 2. Religious tolerance—United States.
3. United States—Religion. I. Title.
BL2525.L554 2010
201'.72—dc22

2010020647

W. W. Norton & Company, Inc.
500 Fifth Avenue, New York, N.Y. 10110
www.wwnorton.com

W. W. Norton & Company Ltd.
Castle House, 75/76 Wells Street, London W1T 3QT

1 2 3 4 5 6 7 8 9 0

For Mark and Kaitlyn

Contents

The Religious Test

Introduction

On the evening of September 12, 1960, John F. Kennedy delivered a speech to the Greater Houston Ministerial Association in which he attempted to defuse a controversy that threatened to derail his presidential campaign—a controversy flowing from the fact of his Catholic faith. In his remarks, Kennedy worked to reassure voters worried about him becoming the nation's first Catholic president, but he also tried to shame his audience, reminding them that Article VI of the US Constitution explicitly stipulates that "no religious Test shall ever be required as a Qualification to any Office or public Trust under the United States." Whereas religious test oaths had been the norm in Europe, compelling office-seekers to affirm a particular religion and excluding members of (in Kennedy's words) "less favored churches" from the exercise of political power, the American constitutional framers had established a political system in which such tests were prohibited. To treat a politician's religious beliefs as politically relevant was thus an affront to "our forefathers" no less than to America's noblest civic traditions—the ones Kennedy himself had "fought for in the South Pacific" and his brother had "died for in Europe" during the Second World War. The candidate's meaning was plain: American ideals demanded that his Catholicism be placed off-limits from public scrutiny.

The speech was an enormous success—and not just because it helped Kennedy win the election. Its more enduring legacy was to convince journalists and other critics not to raise questions about the political implications of specific theological beliefs. In the years since the address, analyzing the dangers of generic "religion" to the nation's political life has remained perfectly acceptable, but evaluating the political predilections of particular religious traditions has come to be seen as simpleminded bigotry. And so we have learned to say—and think—nothing about the subject.

That is a problem, as Kennedy himself implicitly acknowledged in his speech, which did not simply deny the legitimacy of theologically based objections to his candidacy but also answered those objections, directly and forthrightly—making clear that he knew his primary loyalty as president must be to the American people and not to the Vatican. He was right to tackle these concerns head-on. Yes, anti-Catholic prejudice contributed to the nation's concerns about Kennedy's campaign, but prejudice was not their only source. The political history of pre-Vatican II Catholicism—with its overt hostility to democracy, liberalism, toleration, modernity, and religious "error," as well as its emphasis on the absolute authority of the pope in matters of faith and morals—raised perfectly legitimate questions about what it would mean for the United States to elect a Catholic to the nation's highest office. Indeed, widespread apprehensiveness among the American people about such questions showed that they took religious differences more seriously than we do, and that they intuitively understood an important truth that we often forget today—namely, that not all theological assumptions are equally compatible with the political order of the United States.

Kennedy's response to these concerns was to state as bluntly as possible that his faith would play no role in his thinking and actions as president. As he memorably put it, "I do not speak for my church on public matters—and my church does not speak for me." If Kennedy's position had become the norm in the years since his speech—if Americans reliably bracketed their religious convictions when fulfilling their civic duties—then silence about the spiritual beliefs of our fellow citizens and prospective leaders would be perfectly acceptable and appropriate. But alas, the nation has moved in the opposite direction over the past half-century. During these years, and especially since the rise of the religious right in the late 1970s, traditionalist religious believers—those who devote their lives most fully to God and interpret the world in light of a comprehensive system of theological ideas about the nature of reality—have explicitly repudiated Kennedy's stance. As far as many of these devout believers are concerned, citizens and public figures should put their faith at the core of their civic identities and campaigns for political office.

This demands a response—and a new kind of religious test. Unlike the tests proscribed by the Constitution, this one will not threaten to exclude members of specific churches from political participation using formal (or legal) means. In our time of heightened sectarian tensions—when devout believers and secularists increasingly perceive each other to be stationed on opposite sides of a cultural chasm—it is crucially important that the country remain committed to the ideal of active citizenship for all. But defending that ideal does not oblige us to treat the religious views of our fellow citizens with indifference. Quite the reverse: with religion playing an unprecedentedly prominent role in our public life, it is imperative that individuals learn how to do the hard and dirty work of distinguishing between

politically benign and politically toxic forms of religion. That is precisely what the religious test contained in this book will help them to
do—to think wisely, deeply, and above all *critically* about the forms
of religion that have come to play a leading role in our politics and
culture.

My examination of traditionalist religion's diverse challenges to
politics in the United States should not be taken as a sign of antireligious animus. Devout believers have contributed to America's moral
and political development in numerous ways. Quakers, Methodists,
and members of other Protestant denominations were inspired by
their faith to take a risky stand against slavery in the early nineteenth
century, long before most Americans opposed it. Protestant advocates
of the "Social Gospel" helped to inspire such crucially important early-
twentieth-century political movements as Progressivism and the
New Deal. Numerous religious groups, especially black Protestant
churches in the South, launched the civil rights movement of the
1950s and 1960s. Catholic activists have worked tirelessly to allevi-
ate poverty while also contributing in decisive ways to the antiwar
and anti–death penalty movements of recent decades. And then there
is the indisputable connection between piety and philanthropy. As
many studies have shown, regular churchgoers of every denomination contribute significantly more of their income to charity than
their secular counterparts.

All of this is true, and all of it is admirable. But it is not the end of the
story. The fact is that religious convictions do not always harmonize
so pleasingly with the practice of liberal government, and the many
notes of dissonance between them call out for critical attention—and
not merely the kind of attention that comes from a theoretical examination of the separation of church and state. In that our scholars
have excelled, producing countless enlightening studies. Where we
have been less diligent is in exploring the theologically complicated

interrelations between *churches* and state, which is what the rigorous application of the religious test requires. There is, after all, no such thing as "religion" in the abstract. Every religion is radically particular, with its own distinctive claims about God, human history, and the world. These are specific, concrete claims—about the status of the religious community in relation to other groups and to the political community as a whole, about the character of political and spiritual authority, about the place of prophecy in religious and political life, about the proper scope of human knowledge, about the providential role of God in human history, and about the threat that sex and (what is often the same thing) women pose to the social and moral order. These differences matter, and they need to be evaluated.

That the evaluation undertaken in the following chapters consistently judges traditionalist religious beliefs and practices before the bar of political liberalism should not be taken to imply that I advocate bringing those beliefs and practices into conformity with the progressive ideology that dominates the Democratic Party. On the contrary, I use the term *liberal* in a different, explicitly nonideological sense. Just as a monarchy is a system in which one person rules and a theocracy is rule by a class of clerics, *liberalism* is above all a form of government—one in which political rule is mediated by a series of institutions that seek to limit the powers of the state and maximize individual freedom: constitutional government, an independent judiciary, multiparty elections, universal suffrage, a free press, civilian control of the military and police, a large middle class, a developed consumer economy, and rights to free assembly and worship. To be a liberal in this primary sense is to favor a political order with these institutions and to abide by the political rules they establish.

It is also, at an even more fundamental level, to favor these institutions because they comport better than any others with the reality of social and cultural pluralism—with the fact that the United States is riven by deep disagreements about politics and religion. A liberal in this essential sense can be an ideologically committed conservative, moderate, or progressive, just as he can also be a fervent religious traditionalist, a lukewarm believer, an easygoing agnostic, or an ardent atheist. What makes him a political liberal is a habit of mind or temperament linked to the classical virtue of liberality—a willingness to combine an unflinching stand in favor of his own position on a given issue with an attitude of generosity and openness toward those who take a different view. When his favored candidate loses an election or his preferred policy fails to become law, a political liberal accepts the outcome as legitimate, restraining his urge to break the rules of the game, seize political power in the name of his cause, and impose his views on those who dissent from them. These are the basic preconditions of liberal politics and citizenship—preconditions directly tested by many of the ideas and groups on both sides of the religious divide in our country today

It is this conviction—that there is a right way, a liberal way, to behave in the public sphere, and that it is being regularly violated by traditionalist believers and their atheistic antagonists—that has led me to write this book. All of us want, or should want, what is best for our country. All of us want, or should want, to worship God—or not— in peace and freedom. All of us should therefore recognize that we have a shared stake in maintaining the boundaries and distinctions that make peace and freedom possible. In our time, with politics and religion intermingling in ways that are often destructive of both, the habit we most need to foster is one of careful but fearless reflection on precisely where the lines of demarcation between the two parties should be drawn in particular cases. This book is my contribution to that crucially important task.

I

The Imperative
of Religious Freedom

Monotheism—the belief that there is one God—invariably contributes to a sense of distinctiveness. *This* community worships the *true* God; *that* community worships a *false* god. *Our* God is real; *theirs* is an illusion. *We* are saved; *they* are damned. Even Christianity, which at first sight seems to downplay the importance of distinctiveness in favor of a universal ethic, is governed by the particularistic logic of monotheism. Yes, Christians preach a universal faith, but it is a universality based on the infinite expansion of the one true community, which seeks to absorb all other communities into itself through conversion. The history of the West over much of the past two thousand years shows that toward those who refuse to convert—to leave behind their false faiths—Christianity can be very harsh. (The same can be said of Islam.)

This at least partially explains why the Protestant Reformation plunged Europe into sectarian violence. With Christianity broken into two—and soon many more—variants, each considering the others to be based on false beliefs about God, tensions were inevitable. That these tensions repeatedly erupted into mass murder throughout the sixteenth and seventeenth centuries can be traced to the involvement of states in—and the injection of state power into—theological conflict. It's one thing for a believer to think that his neighbor is wrong about God and attempt to convert him to the true view; it's quite another to use organized state power to force conversion. The latter is a recipe for despotism. Unless, of course, the potential convert has different state powers on his side to help him resist and engage in his own program of conversion, in which case civil war is the more likely result.

Caught in seemingly endless cycles of theologically inspired tyranny and civil war, early modern Europe was in desperate need of a rescue operation, and one arrived in the form of an idea—the idea of religious toleration, which took governments out of the conversion business by encouraging them to stop acting as agents of clashing Christian churches. In the liberal politics that flows out of religious toleration, the state strives to stand neutrally above all religious claims. In doing so, government permits each religious group to proselytize, but it also grants (and enforces) the freedom of each group to remain distinctive—to refuse the invitation to convert. The idea of religious toleration obviously contributed in a decisive way to the crafting of the First Amendment to the US Constitution, which protects the free exercise of religion on the part of citizens in large part by precluding the establishment of religion by the federal government. But in time toleration became the norm even in western European countries (like Great Britain) with established churches, where dissenters were eventually granted equal rights to worship and proclaim the gospel in their own distinctive ways without state interference.

State neutrality toward religion has produced enormous benefits, including civil peace and freedom from religious persecution. But it has also generated a new set of problems. The liberal *state* might strive for impartiality in religious matters, but the kind of *society* that grows up under conditions of political freedom is far from being religiously neutral. On the contrary, liberal society puts unprecedented pressures on religion. It fosters spiritual pluralism, which denies any one faith the power to organize the whole of social life. It teaches that public authorities must submit themselves to the consent of those over whom they aspire to rule, thereby undermining the legitimacy of all forms of absolutism. It employs the systematic skepticism of the scientific method to settle important questions of public policy. It encourages the growth of the capitalist marketplace, which unleashes human appetites and gives individuals the freedom to choose among an ever-expanding range of ways to satisfy them. In a liberal society, believers are politically free to practice their faith, but their faith often places them socially on the defensive, fighting a rearguard battle against the cultural, economic, scientific, and political dynamism of modern life.

Confronting these enormous social pressures in recent centuries, many faith communities have chosen to accommodate themselves to the modern dispensation by embracing varying degrees of theological liberalization. But others have set out in the opposite direction— to combat modernity in the name of theological purity. A tension between these alternatives—between liberal religion and antiliberal religion—runs through the history of nearly every modern nation, including the United States. America today, in fact, is home to several highly sectarian religious groups that define themselves in stringent opposition to key aspects of modern life and liberal society. Feeling profoundly threatened, they view radical separation from mainstream society as the only viable path to survival. Indeed, for many, the battle against those who do not hold their beliefs now contributes as much to their identities as the beliefs themselves.

When Americans encounter a member of such groups—an

Amish farmer in the rural Midwest, perhaps, or a Haredi (ultra-Orthodox) Jew on the streets of New York—they may think him oddly dressed, but in most cases they will also take it for granted that it is his birthright as an American to live and worship as he pleases, no matter how far his beliefs diverge from the mainstream. This is as it should be, since liberal toleration demands, at the level of principle, that all believers be permitted to establish, maintain, and pledge loyalty and allegiance to particular subnational communities free from political coercion. But are there any exceptions to this principle? Is a liberal nation obliged in all cases to treat the practices and beliefs of sectarian religious groups with indifference? Or must it instead make distinctions between tolerable and intolerable religious convictions and activities? And if so, where should the lines be drawn? While it may trouble the liberal conscience, it is in fact possible, and indeed necessary, to draw lines on these fundamental matters—to distinguish between groups that do and do not grant their members, as well as society at large, the same religious freedom guaranteed to all.

1

Every year four million tourists travel seventy miles west of Philadelphia on US Route 30 in order to catch a glimpse of another world. Home to roughly one-sixth of the approximately 180,000 Amish who make their homes in rural areas of twenty-four American states and the Canadian province of Ontario, Lancaster County, Pennsylvania, is the Amish capital of the United States in the popular imagination.[1] Thanks in part to the lingering influence of *Witness*, a 1985 Hollywood film set in and around the Amish settlements of Lancaster, tourists flock to the region expecting to see horse-drawn buggies and white-laced bonnets. They are not disappointed. For some, it is a picture of life straight out of the eighteenth century, like Colonial Williamsburg with real-life men, women, and children standing in for the actors. For others, it is a vision of otherworldly Christian purity untouched by the sinful ways of the outside world. The Amish have taken their separatism so far that they've transformed themselves into living museum pieces in the eyes of their fellow citizens—emissaries from an alternative and profoundly foreign reality.

The roots of Amish separatism—including its distinctively anti-political character—go back to its origins as a radical offshoot of the sixteenth-century Protestant Reformation. The forerunners of today's "Pennsylvania Dutch" followed Martin Luther and John Calvin in breaking from the Roman Catholic Church, but they went several steps further, replacing infant baptism with a so-called believer's baptism undertaken by conscious choice later in life (usually in late adolescence), and insisting that all true Christians sever ties to political power. For these "rebaptizers" (or "Anabaptists"), devotion to Christ required renunciation of the force and violence that inevitably prevails in the kingdoms of this world. In its place, Christians were expected to live a life that anticipated the unconditional love that prevails in the kingdom of God—one devoted to peace, nonviolence, and nonresistance to earthly authority.[2]

It was an austere, stringent, and otherworldly form of Protestantism—one that might have died out had the earthly powers that governed northern Europe not undertaken a brutal campaign of persecution against the Anabaptists, thereby confirming their antipolitical convictions and turning large numbers of them into martyrs. By the time their Amish, Mennonite, and Hutterite descendants began to seek refuge in the American colonies during the eighteenth century, the Anabaptist movement had developed into a holistic religious outlook fundamentally predisposed to view modern social and cultural developments with deep suspicion.[3] As the United States modernized around them over the past two centuries, these convictions only intensified.

The Amish do not in fact insist on an absolute rejection of modern conveniences. On the contrary, visitors to their communities are often surprised to discover large Amish-owned businesses, telephone booths standing beside manually plowed fields on deserted dirt roads, and an array of battery- and generator-powered household appliances for sale in town centers. The precise terms of negotiation with the modern world, as well as an array of other social and religious practices, is set by an "order" (*Ordnung*) that defines "the way things are" in a given congregation or church district. When young adults choose to be baptized, they not only publicly declare their Christian faith but also take a vow to uphold the order that prevails among the twenty-five to thirty-five families that constitute their church district.[4] The newly baptized man or woman thus joins a concrete community of neighbors as well as a religion—or rather, he or she joins a concrete community of neighbors fundamentally defined by religion.

Amish religious instruction is remarkably informal. There are no sacred symbols or church buildings (services take place twice a month in private homes), and no traditions of formal religious education. Yet the moral and cultural austerity of Anabaptist Christianity permeates Amish life in countless spoken and unspoken ways, shaping the order of every church district, fundamentally orienting the lives of every individual who vows to uphold it. Every order, for example, aims to instill the virtue of humble "submission" or "self-surrender" (*Gelassenheit*) to the will of God, along with aversion to the sin of high-mindedness or pride (*Hochmut*).[5] Accordingly, every order places severe limits on education, which is thought to instill arrogance and haughty self-regard. "Higher" education is thus unheard of in Amish circles, and even "high" school is usually off-limits.[6] Amish children are taught to read and write, and to master rudimentary mathematics.

But science (beyond "nature study") is strictly forbidden, with books that mention evolution, dinosaurs, or an ice age routinely rejected as unsuitable. One especially conservative community (the Swartzentruber Amish of Holmes County, Ohio) goes so far as to use reprints of *McGuffey's Readers* from 1853 for classroom instruction.[7]

When they discover its stark asceticism, modern Americans often find it difficult to understand how the Amish community manages to perpetuate itself surrounded by a society filled with so many hedonistic temptations. The perplexity deepens when outsiders learn that unlike many separatist groups that severely punish signs of apostasy, most Amish communities routinely give their teenagers considerable latitude to explore the non-Amish world before their baptisms. During this period of "Rumspringa," many Amish teenagers drive cars, listen to radio, watch television, drink alcohol, experiment sexually, and occasionally dabble in drugs and other forms of deviant behavior. After several months or even years of such exploration, however, 90 percent of Amish teenagers definitively reject the outside world by choosing to accept baptism, taking a vow to join the community for the rest of their lives. Once they have taken that vow, they very rarely renege on it.[8]

There is reason to believe that the Amish community's low rate of defections can be traced to its distinctive blend of freedom and constraint. To begin with, the community's premodern mores leave many teenagers ill-prepared to function in or even to make sense of the outside world once they begin to dabble in it.[9] Many of them are profoundly disoriented not only by their first encounter with intense sensory stimulation and sensual pleasure but also by their initial experience of a world dominated by formal institutions, specialization, ethnic and religious diversity, rationalized social relationships, numerous marks of social status, and bureaucratization.[10] For a young adult raised in a tightly knit, homogeneous, egalitarian, and informal community, the simple act of interacting with the modern world can be enough to inspire recoil and an anxious choice to return to the premodern moral and social order of an Amish church district.

For the more adventurous and adaptable, the temptation to make the leap to the modern world is no doubt greater. Yet these teenagers face a monumental decision. Though the Amish tend to be lenient about sinful behavior prior to baptism, they impose a draconian penalty on those who definitively embrace apostasy. Amish who refuse baptism—or who break their baptismal vows later in life—face not just excommunication from a church, but "shunning" (*Meidung*) by the community, which amounts to ostracism from an entire way of life, including rejection by all of one's family and friends. Faced with the threat of expulsion, most young people ultimately return to the fold, however much they may long to escape it.[11]

Then there is the simple fact that young-adult Amish must *choose* to be baptized after having been given the freedom to exit the community—a practice that magnifies the moral gravity of communal membership. Every Amish adult knows that he or she has made a free, informed decision to bind him- or herself for life to God and to the community. Such a promise is much more difficult to break than one entered into out of ignorance or under duress—let alone one tacitly binding from birth or from a baptism undertaken at infancy, before the possibility of consent. In short, the Anabaptist emphasis on freedom of choice—complemented by premodern mores and backed up by severe consequences for the breaking of vows—functions as a remarkably effective mechanism for ensuring the perpetuation of a lifestyle profoundly at odds with the modern world that surrounds it.

But perhaps even more surprising than the capacity of the Amish community to resist modernity is its success at placing itself beyond politics—not just beyond the politics that prevails in American society at large, but beyond politics as such. Virtually alone among separatist groups—indeed, virtually alone among human communities in general—the Amish get along quite well without many of the coercive institutions that civilized human beings take for granted. In the words of sociologist Donald B. Kraybill, the order and discipline that spontaneously prevail in Amish communities lead them to have "little need of external forms of social control—police, courts, prisons." Likewise, "high levels of compliance with traditional Amish values—obedience, hard work, honesty, responsibility, and integrity—means that Amish persons rarely sit in prison for crimes of theft, vandalism, fraud, robbery, or homicide."[12]

As for citizenship—which according to a classical definition involves "ruling and being ruled in turn"—the Amish are content in most cases to allow themselves to be ruled by the state without seeking political rule for themselves. In keeping with their belief in submission, modesty, and self-surrender, they are the ultimate passive citizens. They rarely vote. They pay taxes while opting out of most government social programs. They abide by laws regulating zoning, sanitation, pollution, land use, and childhood vaccination, even though these laws frequently clash with Amish norms and preferences. While their pacifism leads them to conscientiously object to military conscription, they have readily consented to substitute forms of service, often in hospitals far from their communities. There are of course exceptions to Amish passivity in the face of state power. When they feel that the government is infringing on their religious freedom in a fundamental way—as they did, for example, when they fought all the way to the Supreme Court (in *Wisconsin v. Yoder*, 1972) to win the right to take their children out of school in the eighth grade—the Amish can be tenacious adversaries. But for the most part they just want to be left alone to live their lives in devotion to God without external interference of any kind.[13]

And that—along with their use of informal, noncoercive means of enforcing community norms and willingness to grant members permission to peacefully exit the community—is what makes the Amish the ideal separatist group when judged from the standpoint of liberal politics. Liberalism, which limits government power in part to give individuals and groups the freedom to pursue myriad disparate visions of the good, is not threatened by the withdrawal of small numbers of citizens from the day-to-day political, social, and cultural life of the nation.[14] Provided that separatist groups remain small and do not treat their withdrawal as preparation for a future use of state power to impose their sectarian vision of the good on their fellow citizens—provided, in other words, that they keep a consistent distance from politics—their activities and beliefs should be a matter of public indifference. When these groups expand in size or combine the separatist impulse with various forms of illiberal political engagement, however, public indifference can become an act of civic irresponsibility.

2

Secular New Yorkers have been known to refer to the city's many Haredi (ultra-Orthodox) Jews as "urban Amish," and not without reason. Like the Amish, Haredi Jews favor staunch moral traditionalism, including a patriarchal social structure. Members of both groups seek to humble themselves before God by dressing and grooming themselves in an unadorned, monochromatic fashion that starkly sets them apart from outsiders. Just as the Amish accentuate their distinctiveness by speaking an obscure German dialect, so the Haredim often choose to speak Yiddish within their homes and businesses while, like many less punctiliously observant Jews, reverting to Hebrew for worship and prayer. And finally, each sect prefers to live in a homogeneous community as insulated as possible from the aspects of modernity that it finds most threatening to its own form of piety.

The story of how a faction of Judaism forged a way of life so similar to the one cultivated by a radical band of Anabaptist Protestants goes back several centuries. Haredi Judaism originated in central and eastern Europe as a traditionalist reaction by Ashkenazi Jews against the eighteenth-century Enlightenment and its promise of Jewish emancipation. Numerous writers associated with the Enlightenment (including such prominent Jews as Moses Mendelssohn) advocated the end of enforced Jewish segregation and the granting of full political rights to Jews—provided that they embraced the ideal of assimilation into the Christian cultures of Europe. Although in most cases Jews were not required formally to convert to Christianity, the often unspoken presumption throughout post-Enlightenment Europe was that in return for emancipation Jews would downplay their distinctiveness, "blending in" as much as possible, easing their observance of rituals that had defined Judaism throughout the past several centuries of the diaspora.[15]

A pair of movements grew up in opposition to the promise of emancipation. The first, Hasidism, emerged toward the end of the eighteenth century in the communities of Podolia and Volhynia in present-day Ukraine and quickly spread throughout central and eastern Europe. Emphasizing the mystical tradition of Kabbalah, Hasidic piety was deeply anti-intellectual, focusing its religious fervor on the leadership of a charismatic rabbi who came to be seen as an almost messianic redeemer. The second movement, Lithuanian Misnagdism, arose in explicit opposition to Hasidism's ecstatic style of worship, insisting instead on the crucial importance of Talmudic scholarship in the life of the Jewish community and treating great learning as the mark of a true leader. Despite these fundamental points of disagreement, the two movements were united in rejecting the legitimacy of assimilation into the gentile cultures surrounding them.[16]

By the late nineteenth and early twentieth centuries, with Jews throughout Europe learning vernacular languages, moving out of ghettos, dressing in fashionable clothes, and attending universities, followers of Hasidism and Misnagdism began to recognize that their similarities vastly outweighed their differences. Against the ideal of assimilation, the groups championed a stark alternative: a life of deliberate Jewish insularity tightly orbiting around intense study of Torah, Mishnah, and Talmud, and fortified by the strictest possible observance of Jewish law and ritual.[17] These are the rudiments of what is known today as Haredism. The word is derived from the Hebrew for "fear" or "anxiety"—Haredi Jews are those who are anxiously religious or who tremble before God (Isaiah 66:2, 5)—though they more often refer to themselves simply as "*Yidn*" (Jews) or "*erlicher Yidn*" (virtuous Jews), highlighting their conviction that they are the only true Jews.[18] This form of Judaism would champion what one of its early exemplars, the rabbi Avraham Karelitz, called the "sweetness of extremism." "He who champions a middle course and scorns extremism," Karelitz declared, "has a place among the counterfeiters, with those lacking wisdom. If there is no extremism, there is no completeness."[19]

Haredi pessimism about the possibility of a rapprochement between Judaism and modernity seemed vindicated by the Holocaust, in which the Haredi Jews of central and eastern Europe perished at far higher rates than more secular and assimilated Jews. The very distinctiveness of the Haredim made them easy and obvious targets for the Nazis and their collaborators across the region. The bulk of Haredi survivors nonetheless emerged from the Shoah more convinced than ever that the survival of Judaism under modern conditions, as well as the commemoration of millions of deaths at the hands of gentiles, required radical separation from and antagonism to the non-Haredi world. In practice, this meant the strictest possible religious observance, intense devotion to religious study in exclusively Jewish schools (yeshivas), and the choice to live in homogeneous enclaves with other Haredi Jews.[20]

In the contemporary United States, Haredi Jews are a minority within a minority within a minority. Depending on the criteria used by demographers, there are between 5 and 7 million Jews in the country, which amounts to 2 to 3 percent of the population. Of those 5 to 7 million, an estimated 700,000—or roughly 10 to 13 percent—can be described as Orthodox in observance. Yet Orthodoxy itself is divided between the so-called modern Orthodox, who attempt to combine strict religious observance with full participation in modern American life, and Haredi Jews, who embrace parochialism and refuse any accommodation with modernity. Indications are that the Haredi population matches or slightly surpasses that of the Amish—totaling between 188,000 and 207,000, according to the careful calculations of sociologist Samuel C. Heilman.[21]

Yet Haredism is growing. Not only does the sexual traditionalism of Haredi Jews lead them to have much larger families than less fervently observant Jews, but they have also been quite successful in persuading adherents of modern Orthodoxy to move rightward in recent decades. Much of this influence has come through the practice of *Kiruv*, a form of intra-Jewish outreach that amounts to proselytism. Especially among the children of the modern Orthodox, such efforts not infrequently inspire curiosity about and conversion to the stricter forms of observance and separatist practices of the Haredim. Appalled by high rates of intermarriage between Jews and gentiles, as well as by what they perceive to be an increasingly sleazy and insidious popular culture, these kids often prove to be an ideal audience for the argument that Judaism's best hope for survival lies in withdrawal from modern America and the embrace of exclusivity and insularity.[22]

The growth of Haredism can be seen in its expansion out of its historic American home in Brooklyn, New York. Although the single largest concentration of Haredi Jews in the United States continues to be found in Brooklyn (where 75,000 make their home), recent decades have witnessed explosive growth of Haredism in a handful of towns and villages throughout the New York metropolitan area. Relatively small homogeneous Haredi communities (each with fewer than 13,000 residents) can be found in the towns of Kiryas Joel, New Square, and Kaser in upstate New York. The town of Monsey, New York, is home to a larger community of 20,000 Haredim, 6,000 of whom speak only Yiddish. Even larger and more densely populated is the town of Lakewood, New Jersey, where 38,000 Haredi Jews make their home within a mile radius of a huge yeshiva and its associated religious institutions.[23]

Surprisingly, Haredi Jews have even begun to move into the religiously heterogeneous suburbs of New York, Philadelphia, and Chicago—though they have done so in their own distinctive way. Viewing suburbanization as one of many trends leading the bulk of American Jews into apostasy, the Haredim have tended to resist numerous hallmarks of suburban life, including reliance on cars and indifference to the religious makeup of neighborhoods.[24] When the Haredim relocate to the suburbs, they tend to move in groups of several families, clustering into neighborhoods within walking distance of an ultra-Orthodox synagogue that serves as an anchor for a suburban settlement. Walkability is crucial because of Sabbath restrictions on the use of automobiles. Similar considerations have led some neighborhoods to move even further in the direction of self-segregation, encircling themselves with an *ervu chatzayrot*—a wire (usually strung between utility poles) that encloses several Haredi homes, joining them into a common "private" space within which the Torah-based prohibition against carrying items between public and private domains on the Sabbath does not apply.[25]

Such practices, which amount to the deliberate revival and self-imposition of Old World ghettoization, give concrete expression to the drive for separatism that lies at the heart of Haredi identity. The Haredim believe it is crucial for "true" Jews to reject the pluralism that dominates the United States in favor of an insular life devoted exclusively to following God's law with perfect exactitude and building a radically homogeneous "scholars' society" unwaveringly oriented toward religious worship. In nearly all respects, this exclusivist social vision stands in stark contrast to the customs and ideals that prevail among most of their fellow citizens—including non-Haredi Jews.[26]

Most twenty-first-century Americans may consider these attitudes strange, but they are unlikely to see them as a threat to the country at large, and rightly so. To be sure, unlike the explicitly antipolitical Amish, Haredi Jews do vote, often as a bloc, and nearly always with the interests of the Haredi community as their primary consideration.[27] Yet their political influence is negligible outside the handful of munici-palities where they constitute a majority of voters, and it is likely to stay that way, even as their numbers grow over the coming years. As the Haredim are well aware, the United States is, demographically speak-ing, an overwhelmingly Christian nation in which they are a minuscule minority with no realistic prospects for bringing the country into con-formity with their way of life. Like the Amish, then, though for more pragmatic reasons, the Haredim show little interest in pursuing politi-cal rule—beyond, of course, defending their right to worship God as they choose, without external interference.[28]

This is not to say that there are no points of tension between Haredi customs and the nation's liberal political order. On the contrary, such tensions exist and are likely to grow over time, as the Haredim take increasing advantage of the American legal tradition's willingness to grant religious groups the freedom to govern their own affairs using what are called "alternative forms of dispute resolution" (ADR). The most prominent institution serving as an ADR for the Haredi community is the Beth Din of America—a rabbinical court that adjudicates commercial, communal, and familial financial disputes, as well as handling divorces, child custody, and "personal status" cases (that is, establishing who is and who is not a Jew, whether a marriage conforms to the requirements of Jewish law, and so forth). In keeping with common American practice, the Beth Din's rulings are legally binding and enforceable in the civil court system.

The custom of granting legal authority to religiously based forms of ADR, along with the "free exercise" clause of the First Amendment, helps to make the United States a world leader in defending the right of religious freedom. Yet the practice also poses difficult questions for liberal politics, most of them flowing from the fact that members of religious groups possess inviolable rights as American citizens that may conflict with the (different and often more limited) rights recognized by religious institutions. What if one of the parties to a dispute—a woman seeking to dissolve an arranged marriage to an abusive husband, for example—claims to have entered into her marriage contract, along with its stipulation that marital disputes will be resolved by rabbinical ADR, under duress? Normally civil courts dissolve contracts in which one of the parties can prove he or she was coerced into agreement. But who decides what counts as coercion? The religious group? Or the civil courts? Must there be an explicit threat of violence? Or do more subtle but no less threatening forms of communal pressure meet the standard?

And what about cases in which the religious community and American law differ on what counts as a civil as opposed to a criminal matter? Has a husband in a traditionalist religious community who routinely beats his wife committed a crime? Or is he merely fulfilling his God-given duty to rule over his household as he sees fit? More precisely, does respect for the religious freedom of Haredi Jews require that the civil courts allow such matters to be adjudicated by rabbis applying Jewish law (Halacha), even if that law diverges in fundamental respects from American law? And what if the traditionalists are not Jews but devout Muslims seeking to abide by the tenets of Islamic law (Sharia)? Should American civil courts enforce a contract that calls for disputes between two Muslim American citizens to be resolved by an imam following the laws of theocratic Saudi Arabia?

3

Though many Americans would no doubt be surprised by the news, American law already permits precisely this. Indeed, civil courts in several states, including New Jersey, Minnesota, and Texas, have already upheld and enforced such contracts without controversy.[29] The same cannot be said for some of America's closest allies. Although England, like the United States, allows Jews to set up institutions to arbitrate disputes, a proposal by Rowan Williams (the Anglican Archbishop of Canterbury) to expand these rights to Muslims provoked a storm of controversy on both sides of the Atlantic during the winter of 2008, with critics charging that such a move would effectively create an illiberal "'state within a state' in which the writ of secular legislation hardly runs at all."[30] The uproar in the UK followed an earlier and longer-lasting conflagration in the Canadian province of Ontario between 2003 and 2005, when a retired lawyer, Syez Mumtaz Ali, attempted to set up a Sharia-based civil court under the province's 1991 Arbitration Act and then was blocked from doing so after public figures from across the political and religious spectrum weighed in against it.[31]

Are there any reasonable grounds for discriminating against Muslims in this way? Is it simply blind prejudice, a blatant double standard, to assert that rights granted to Haredi Jews should be denied to Muslims? Or is there something distinctive about Muslim separatism—the ideas and attitudes that inspire it, perhaps, or maybe the much larger size of the Muslim community in Great Britain compared with the minuscule number of Haredi Jews in the country—that makes it a greater threat to the liberal political order than Jewish separatism? And if so, is this threat the same in all liberal nations? More specifically, is the American tendency to allow all religious groups, including Muslims, to make use of ADR an admirable mark of open-mindedness? Or is it instead a sign of foolishness, a vivid example of the dangerous consequences of giving religious convictions, no matter how illiberal, the benefit of the doubt?

The most important thing to be noted about Muslim piety is that, at least at the present moment in history, it is distinctive in two politically significant respects. For one thing, an indeterminate number of Muslims around the world adhere to a virulently antiliberal ideology of political conquest and absolute rule known variously as Wahhabism and Salafism.[32] While it is unlikely that any more than a small number of American Muslims sympathize with Wahhabist and Salafist ideas, the radical incompatibility of these ideas with liberal government and the proclivity of their most passionate proponents to advocate the use of terrorist violence against civilians produces justified anxiety among the citizens of free societies all over the world, but especially in the United States, England, Spain, and other countries where Islamic terrorists have struck in recent years. In this respect, Islam is quite different from and potentially much more threatening to the liberal political order than either Anabaptist Christianity or Haredi Judaism.

This points to the second significant example of Muslim distinctiveness. Whereas the Amish and Haredim are fundamentalist dissenters from the well-developed liberal traditions that dominate their respective religions, Islam has (as yet) no organized, institutionally grounded liberal tradition. To be sure, there are liberal imams scattered throughout the United States; if a Muslim who dissents from traditionalism is lucky enough to find him- or herself in the vicinity of a mosque with more moderate leanings, theological liberalism might be an option. But for most Muslims there is no such option. The vast majority of America's roughly 1,300 mosques and several hundred religious schools are highly conservative, separating the sexes for worship and assigning subordinate roles to women. Moreover, in the words of scholar Paul M. Barrett, "most observant Muslims view the Koran as the literal word of God, not a work of divine inspiration composed by humans, as most observant Jews and Christians describe their scriptures." When it comes to cultural views, "two-thirds of American Muslims consider the United States 'immoral' because of permissive attitudes toward sex outside marriage and toward alcohol, both of which Islam bans," and (like many conservative Christians) most likewise favor outlawing pornography, support public funding for religious schools, and strenuously oppose abortion and homosexuality.[33] To be an observant Muslim is in most cases to be a traditionalist Muslim. And that means that more liberal Muslims often confront a stark choice: either embrace one of several forms of theological orthodoxy or else break from the faith to embrace secularism.

The default traditionalism of observant Muslims is in part what lies behind the recent controversies in Great Britain and Canada about granting Muslim communities the right to employ judicially sanctioned methods of ADR. If a Haredi Jew wishes to exit her community, she can always seek refuge among less fervent Jews—whether they be modern Orthodox, conservative, reformed, reconstructionist, or humanistic in theological orientation. That might not be possible for a Muslim apostate. Moreover, because apostasy is a punishable offense under Sharia law, a Muslim woman seeking to avoid physical abuse, genital mutilation, or forced marriage faces the added fear of vigilante violence.[34] It is the presence of these formidable obstacles to exiting the Islamic community that lead many to oppose granting ADR rights to Muslims. These critics rightly insist that the liberal state has a special obligation to ensure that potential victims of theologically inspired violence and other forms of abuse have recourse to the protections of civil and criminal law.

But the extraordinary intensity of the reaction in Canada and Great Britain to seemingly modest ADR proposals points to broader fears— some of them well-founded—about the place of Muslims within the liberal societies of western Europe. Whereas the Amish and Haredi communities of the United States each constitute less than 0.1 percent of the American population, Muslims make up approximately 2.8 percent of the British population, 3 percent of the German population, 5.8 percent of the Dutch population, and 9 percent of the French population.[35] And the Muslim communities of western Europe are not only relatively large; they also tend to be economically impoverished, poorly educated, and socially marginalized. This marginalization is exacerbated by the generous welfare benefits common on the European continent, which "allow Muslims and other immigrants to live indefinitely on the periphery of society, without steady jobs or social interaction with the majority."[36] And then there is the legacy of colonialism, which leads the Muslim communities of Europe to be isolated and inward-looking, with members speaking a single foreign language and united by distinct ethnic identities. All of these structural factors encourage the separatist tendencies of Muslims living in Europe and contribute to their political radicalization, creating an environment in which advocates of the violently illiberal Wahhabist and Salafist ideologies can find eager recruits.

Despite a handful of cases in which American Muslims have attempted to perpetrate acts of terrorism, the overall situation of Muslims in the United States is significantly more encouraging than it is in Europe. America's Muslim community is not only smaller than those in most European countries—at 2 to 3 million people, it constitutes roughly 1 to 2 percent of the population—but it is also more ethnically diverse. Thirty-four percent of American Muslims come from South Asia (Pakistan, India, Bangladesh, and Afghanistan), while 26 percent hail from Arab countries, with the remainder divided among native-born African Americans and immigrants from Africa, Turkey, Iran, and elsewhere. Moreover, far from wallowing in poverty, American Muslims have a median family income of $60,000, substantially exceeding the national average of roughly $50,000, as does the percentage of Muslims holding college degrees (59 percent compared with 27 percent of all Americans).[37]

As for Muslim integration into the political culture of the United States, it has been facilitated by the country's willingness to tolerate a vibrant role for religion in public life—and in particular by the Republican Party's strenuous efforts since the 1970s to attract socially and religiously conservative voters of any and every denomination. While the right wing of the GOP likes to flirt with illiberalism, it remains a center-right party firmly situated within the American political mainstream. Republicans deserve credit for drawing Muslims out of religiously homogeneous enclaves, where they might be tempted to embrace far more virulent and deadly ideologies, to actualize their citizenship by participating in politics.

At least that's the way integration was proceeding prior to the terrorist attacks of September 11, 2001. Since then, the trends have been less encouraging. George W. Bush's extremely aggressive response to the attacks—launching wars against two Muslim nations along with authorizing the arrest, detention, interrogation, and (in some cases) torture of more than 9,000 Muslim and Arab men—made many Muslims feel unwelcome in the United States in general and in the Republican Party in particular.[38] This is unfortunate—and not only because in many cases the government's actions have been unjust. President Bush's actions should be lamented because they threatened to reproduce in the United States the pathological social patterns so common in western Europe—namely, Muslim withdrawal from mainstream political and cultural life and subsequent embrace of ideological radicalism.[39] Call it one of many unintended consequences of the "global war on terror."

Faced with this tense new reality, the United States should pursue a moderate course. On the one hand, we need to step down from our aggressive war footing and refuse to reward public officials for employing morally irresponsible (and intellectually sloppy) rhetoric about the existential threat of "Islamofascism."[40] On the other hand, we must insist that Muslim communities conform to the moral norms of modern America—above all in allowing its members exit without penalty. While Muslims should be permitted to continue using forms of ADR, their arbitration agreements (like those of Haredi Jews and other religious groups) should be carefully and stringently regulated by civilian courts to ensure that the parties abide by the kinds of constraints routinely enforced in civil contracts. Given the unique and subtle forms of coercion that can come into play in separatist religious communities, civil judges need to be especially vigilant in looking for signs of duress on the part of those granted the fewest rights within the community (in most cases, women and children). Lastly, in deciding whether or not to enforce a contract, civil judges need to be closely attuned to America's constantly evolving legal consensus on where the line between civil and criminal law should be drawn. A twenty-first-century American woman who is physically abused by her husband needs to know she has recourse to the laws of the liberal state, regardless of whether the arcane statutes of Halacha or Sharia recognize the act as a criminal offense.

4

Islam is by no means the only religion in the United States in which a small minority is consumed by a radical political theology. What Wahhabism and Salafism are to the Muslim community, Christian Reconstructionism is to Christianity—a tiny sect whose extremism gives the faith of less radical believers a bad name while posing a genuine threat to the country at large.[41] In stark contrast to the largely antipolitical Amish, Reconstructionists believe that Christians are called to absolute political rule, which they describe in ominous terms as "dominion under God." Unlike the Haredim, who long to be left alone to worship God in peace, Reconstructionists believe in overturning the political and cultural order of modern America, which they consider an abomination. Whereas mainstream Muslims have worked in concert with social conservatives of other faiths to advance an interreligious public policy agenda, Reconstructionists hope to establish a Christian theocracy in the United States—a regime in which apostasy, along with homosexuality, will be punishable by death. It is no exaggeration to describe Reconstructionists as the Taliban of American Christianity.

But there is a crucial difference between the place of Muslim and Christian extremists in the United States. While the audience for radical Islam is mostly limited to the roughly 2 percent of Americans who are observant Muslims, the pool of potential recruits to Reconstructionism is vastly larger. Not that many Christians, even on the religious right, are likely to be persuaded explicitly to join the Reconstructionist ranks, an act that would take them quite far outside the American mainstream. Yet, as recent books by Michelle Goldberg and Kevin Phillips have amply documented, Reconstructionism has left a significant mark on the political outlook of conservative evangelicals, many of whom have (perhaps unknowingly) assimilated a number of its most heterodox ideas about American history, culture, and politics.[42] As long as this influence continues, Reconstructionism deserves to be considered a small but significant threat to the liberal political order of the United States.

Christian Reconstructionism traces its roots to 1864 and the founding of the National Reform Association (NRA), an organization of staunchly conservative Calvinists who hoped to stem the tide of secularism in the mid-nineteenth-century United States by lobbying for an explicitly Christian amendment to the US Constitution. Convinced that the bloody battlefields of the Civil War as well as the dislocations of economic and technological modernization flowed from the absence of references to God and Jesus Christ in the nation's founding document, the members of the NRA sought to placate the deity by persuading their fellow citizens to revise it. The NRA's 1890 proposal for a Christian constitutional amendment nicely captures its longstanding intent:

> [We petition] . . . for such an Amendment to the Constitution of the United States as shall suitably express our national acknowledgement of Almighty God as the source of all authority in civil government; of the Lord Jesus Christ as the Ruler of nations and of His revealed will as the supreme standard to decide moral issues in national life, and thus indicate that this is a Christian nation, and place all the Christian laws, institutions, and usages of the government on an undeniably legal basis in the fundamental law of the land.[43]

Needless to say, such an amendment would dramatically alter the Constitution, transforming it from a document establishing popular

sovereignty ("We the People . . .") to one that publicly declares political authority to derive from the Christian God. This would seem to
entail the establishment of Calvinist Christianity as America's state
religion, and the reduction of non-Christians (and perhaps also non-
Calvinist Christians) to the status of second-class citizens. It would
be, in other words, a significant step on the road to establishing a
theocracy in America.

The United States has never come close to adopting such an
amendment. But the intense religious passions that first motivated
the NRA to propose it have not disappeared. Countless preachers and
theologians have given voice to them over the years, though perhaps
none more compellingly or influentially than Rousas John (R. J.)
Rushdoony, Christian Reconstructionism's founding father. Drawing
on the political theology of Abraham Kuyper, the founder of Dutch
Calvinism, Rushdoony asserted that, rightly understood, the Bible
encourages active civic engagement on the part of Christians. From
the Christian apologetics of philosopher Cornelius Van Til he drew
the lesson that all worldviews, including secular ones, are founded
in a rationally inexplicable act of faith—and thus that Christians are
perfectly justified in assuming, without evidence or argument, the
infallible, comprehensive truth of the Bible. And from theologian
Francis A. Schaeffer he absorbed the view that authentic Christianity
in the United States has been supplanted by a demonic counter-faith
of secular humanism that is eating away at the "whole structure of
our society"—and that it is the duty of devout believers to reestablish
a robust public presence for intense Christian piety.[44]

Synthesizing these radical positions, Rushdoony boldly declared
that Christians are empowered by God to save the United States by
exercising "dominion"—that is, by rising to positions of political rule
from which the civil and criminal laws of the state may be used to
shape the consciences of citizens. In this respect, Reconstructionism

is a form of separatism with a difference: it views withdrawal from the corruptions of modern America as a prelude to and preparation for a final battle to retake cultural and political territory from the forces of darkness. For a Christian to settle for anything less—including accommodation with liberal pluralism and toleration—is unthinkable, a blasphemous affront to God, who intends human law to be used exclusively to form and strengthen "Christian man and Christian society." Indeed, in Rushdoony's view, "nothing is more deadly and more derelict than the notion that the Christian is at liberty with respect to the kind of law he can have." American Christians are therefore called to "reconstruct" their nation and its political system along explicitly Christian lines—to bring it into complete conformity with a fundamentalist understanding of the Bible and God's plan for the human race.[45]

Today Rushdoony's ideas are most closely associated with the Presbyterian Church in America (PCA), which broke off from the mainline Presbyterian Church–USA in December 1973 over its growing theological liberalism.[46] As of 2007, the Atlanta-based PCA claimed 345,582 "communicant and non-communicant" members, as well as 1,666 churches and missions, in the United States and Canada.[47] Whether all or even most PCA members endorse Rushdoony's dominionist theology is anyone's guess.

What we do know is that numerous evangelical preachers and organizations affiliated with other denominations have worked to spread Rushdoony's ideas over the past few decades. Rushdoony's son-in-law Gary North wrote in 1981 about the need for activists to penetrate secular institutions to "smooth the transition to Christian political leadership," and in subsequent years he has contributed to this goal by selling books online that advocate "theonomic rule"—that is, a system of government under divine law.[48] Rushdoony protégé Gary DeMar—who considers "the modern concept of pluralism" to be "one of the most pernicious inventions of the twentieth century designed to eliminate the Christian religion"—has worked with like-minded believers to disseminate Reconstructionist educational materials to Christian churches and institutions.[49] And then there is the late D. James Kennedy, who decisively contributed to the spread of Reconstructionist ideas by founding Coral Ridge Ministries in 1974. Through its two branches (the Center for Reclaiming America for Christ and the Center for Christian Statesmanship) and its television show (*The Coral Ridge Hour*), which reportedly reaches an audience of 3.5 million, the organization seeks to bring God's "truth and His will to bear on every sphere of our world and our society." In Kennedy's view, which echoed Rushdoony's, devout Christians must "exercise godly dominion and influence over our neighborhoods, our schools, our government . . . our entertainment media, our news media, our scientific endeavors—in short, over every aspect and institution of human society."[50]

5

In no area of contemporary American life have these radical religious ideas had greater (and more insidious) effect than in the explosive growth of the home-schooling movement over the past thirty-five years. The trend of pulling children out of the public school system to be educated at home by parents (nearly always mothers) actually began on the left side of the political–cultural spectrum, with the publication of Jim Holt's *How Children Fail* in 1970. Assuming the inherent goodness of children and advocating their liberation from the tyranny of "experts" that supposedly ruled the bureaucratically stultifying public schools, Holt inspired several thousand anti-authoritarian counterculturalists to "unschool" their children by giving them maximum freedom to pursue their studies at home.[51]

Had it remained an expression of left-wing populism, the home-schooling movement might have died out or remained as marginal as the hippie-dominated commune movement of the late sixties. But by the early 1980s, home-schooling was being championed by a very different kind of parent—one who was motivated to home-school not by the authoritarianism of the public education system but rather by its secular liberalism. Encouraged by the writings of Seventh Day Adventist and education researcher Raymond Moore, which were heavily promoted by such heroes of the religious right as James Dobson and Phyllis Schlafly, these Christian conservatives became convinced that their "instinctual" knowledge as parents entitled them to take full responsibility for the education of their children, including insulating them from the morally and religiously corrosive skepticism that supposedly permeated the public schools.[52]

Most of the explosive growth in home-schooling over the past twenty-five years—from roughly 50,000 children in 1983 to roughly 1.5 million, or 2.9 percent of all American students, in 2007—can be traced to the enthusiasm of Christian conservatives.[53] Today about 80 percent of home-schooled kids identify as evangelical Protestant, with the remaining 20 percent made up of post-hippie "free schoolers" and sundry Catholics, mainline Protestants, Mormons, Jehovah's Witnesses, Muslims, Buddhists, Taoists, and members of more marginal religious groups.[54] Some parents home-school their kids because their local schools are inferior. Others do it because of their kids' bad experiences with bullying peers or abusive teachers. But the statistical evidence indicates the vast majority of parents choose to home-school for religious and moral reasons—as a way of protecting their children from the dangers of the "outside" world.

The motives of evangelical home-schoolers are thus quite similar to those of other separatist groups. Yet home-schooling separatism is unique—and uniquely troubling. Evangelical home-schoolers have no objection to automobiles and most others forms of technology. Though they may choose to dress modestly, they do not reject modern fashion on principle. They abide by no distinctive set of divine laws regulating conduct within the community and between the community and the wider world. They do not punish apostasy or preclude exit. Indeed, with few exceptions, they consider the laws of the United States to be perfectly compatible with their faith, provided they are interpreted correctly.

Therein lies the distinctiveness of their separatism. Evangelical home-schoolers tend to perceive themselves not merely as *true Christians*, which would make them quite similar to members of other separatist religious groups, but also as *true Americans*. Their separatism exists right alongside modern, pluralistic America, in a kind of parallel universe. This alternative America *looks* very much like the contemporary United States, but it *feels* very different, with conservative evangelical piety permeating every aspect of life. Not so much a withdrawal or escape from the American experience, evangelical separatism must be understood as an effort to spiritualize and sanctify the American experience from the inside.

To get a sense of the proximity of the home-schooling movement to modern American life, one need only ponder the role that grassroots political activism and entrepreneurial ambition have played in its rapid growth. When the movement began, nearly every state expected children to attend school outside the home, sometimes explicitly, through mandatory attendance laws, and sometimes by implication, through teacher-certification requirements. By 1992, twenty-five states had changed these laws.[55] The following year brought an even bigger victory, with the Michigan Supreme Court recognizing a right to home-school under the First Amendment and definitively knocking down teacher-certification requirements.[56] Today there are effectively no legal obstacles to home-schooling anywhere in the United States.

Home-schoolers owe these rapid changes primarily to the efforts of one man, Michael Farris, founder of the Home School Legal Defense Association (HSLDA) and its lobbying arm, the Congressional Action Program (CAP). The movement was still in its infancy in 1981 when Farris, a lawyer and Christian activist in Washington state, decided that he and his wife would try home-schooling their children. Immediately convinced of its importance for raising devout Christians, Farris founded the HSLDA the following year in the hope of making it easier for evangelical families to separate themselves from the public schools, which he described as "godless monstrosities" and the leading edge of a "multibillion-dollar inculcation machine" designed to spread "secular humanism and New Age religions" throughout the nation. Convinced that the public schools were a "far more dangerous propaganda machine than existed in the Soviet Union," Farris claimed that they were guilty of "destroying continuing generations of children" and planned to use his organization to stop them.[57] The Michigan ruling eleven years later was its greatest triumph.

The spread of Christian home-schooling has been facilitated by the creation of an industry that produces a huge selection of educational materials for parents who wish to teach their children at home. Whether this material benefits students is notoriously difficult to gauge. On the one hand, most standardized forms of assessment show that home-schooled kids acquire the same cognitive skills and learn much of the same basic information as those who attend school outside the home. Indeed, home-schoolers tend to score at or slightly above the national average on the SAT and similar tests.[58] On the other hand, many of the textbooks and teaching aids produced for Christian home-schoolers seem designed to make it possible for parents to raise their children to adulthood in a traditionalist-Christian cocoon. Whereas a child educated in the public schools would likely learn that most of the American constitutional framers were Episcopalian

deists who opposed the creation of an established church, a child educated at home using the popular A Beka Book curriculum program
would be taught that the American founders were pious Christians
who believed that only the similarly devout could be considered good
citizens. They might also learn that God very much supported the
founders in their efforts—and that He opposes those in our time who
propose a different interpretation of the historical record. A Beka's
God's World series of science books likewise assumes the literal validity of the Genesis creation story and dismisses the findings of evolutionary biology. And so it goes, through textbooks on physics, sex
education, foreign languages, and much else—providing a unified
evangelical Protestant view of everything under the sun.[59]

This points to an even more worrying aspect of evangelical home-
schooling. Early critics of the movement worried that children educated at home would become social misfits lacking the rudimentary
interpersonal skills that kids normally acquire through everyday interaction with peers in school. We now know that such concerns were
largely misplaced. In most cases, parents of home-schooled children
organize groups in order to provide their kids with a social outlet.
With rare exceptions, children educated at home are neither isolated
nor socially stunted.

Whether they are civically stunted is another matter. Children educated at home for religious purposes might be provided with a peer
group by their parents, but as long as that peer group consists entirely
of other home-schooled kids, it will be severely constricted. By hap-
hazardly throwing together kids from various ethnic, racial, socioeconomic, and religious backgrounds, public and private schools tacitly
teach important lessons in liberal citizenship—lessons in toleration,
human diversity, mutual respect, and the complicated realities of social
pluralism. Even when the school performs this function poorly—in
racially and economically homogeneous inner-city classrooms, for

example, or in the pristine halls of uniformly wealthy prep schools—it will still expose its students to a broader range of human types than a child taught at home for religious reasons is likely to encounter.[60] Terrified of the pluralism that permeates modern America, insistent on exercising complete control over the peer interactions of their children, convinced that the schools are filled with virulent forms of "social contagion" from which their kids need to be quarantined, evangelical home-schoolers go out of their way to ensure that their children are insulated from the experiences that help to form habits of liberal citizenship.[61] Like all religious separatists, in other words, Christian home-schoolers hope to raise children who live in but are not of modern America.

At least as modern America is currently constituted. Many home-schoolers dream of transforming the nation into a different place—a place where their own brand of fervent piety will set the political and cultural tone and no longer be forced to adopt a merely defensive stance on the periphery of American public life. For those truly committed to this insurgent agenda, eighteen years of inoculation against the outside world is insufficient. It must be supplemented by several years of spiritual combat training to turn their children into crusaders for Christ, prepared to defeat the forces of darkness and redeem the nation in the name of God.

It was this vision of home-schoolers as an elite core of spiritual shock troops—the Army Rangers of the culture war—that motivated Michael Farris to found Patrick Henry College in 2000. Located on a hundred-acre campus an hour from Washington DC in the northern Virginia suburb of Purcellville, Patrick Henry has been dubbed "Harvard for Home-schoolers." Farris himself likes to speak of its students as the "Joshua Generation"—the generation that, like the biblical Joshua, will lead the chosen people to the promised land after years of suffering and struggle in the desert. Accordingly, the school hopes to turn out graduates "who, because they love God, refuse to sit silently by while their nation hates what He loves and loves what He hates."[62] As journalist Hanna Rosin has noted in her illuminating portrait of the school, students at Patrick Henry view it as their divine mission to "shape the culture and take back the nation." Indeed, "their parents whisper it in their ears like a secret destiny: *There's a world out there, a lost and fallen world, and you alone can rescue it.*"[63]

Students at Patrick Henry prepare to fulfill these theological–political expectations by combining extensive internships inside the Washington Beltway with the study of classic texts—though their classroom experience can hardly be described as a liberal arts education. Farris personally insists that students treat their study of Plato, Aristotle, Locke, Virgil, Shakespeare, and Milton as "opposition research" and mandates that faculty must "regularly affirm the Bible as the ultimate source of all truth" in every single class.[64] These strictures are so severe that a number of the most popular members of the Patrick Henry faculty, all of them conservative evangelicals, resigned or were fired in the spring of 2006 for daring to teach such authors as Augustine and Immanuel Kant without focusing entirely on their errors. In search of a more open academic atmosphere, two of these scholars (Robert Stacey and Erik Root) chose to relocate to Pat Robertson's Regent University.[65]

The character and quality of the education at Patrick Henry has so far been no obstacle to the political ambitions of its students. On the contrary, they have been remarkably successful at landing high-profile internships with conservatives in Congress, the White House, and various departments of the executive branch, often beating out applicants from some of the most prestigious (but liberal-leaning) schools in the country. Indeed, their prevalence in Washington during the administration of George W. Bush seemed to indicate that Patrick Henry's students—unwaveringly loyal, intellectually incurious, morally absolutist, religiously fervent, ideologically doctrinaire—are quite welcome within the present incarnation of the Republican Party.[66]

It's hard to see what good can come from such a movement. In actively seeking to perpetuate their own parochialism, evangelical home-schoolers are no different than the Amish, Haredi Jews, and many other sectarian groups. Yet unlike most such groups, who merely wish to preserve themselves in a spiritually inhospitable environment, evangelical Protestants who choose to educate their children at home often have missionary motives, which at least partially accounts for the movement's explosive growth over the past three decades. A society of 300 million people can afford to permit a handful of separatist groups, each numbering a few hundred thousand, to live and worship as they wish. But how about a rapidly expanding movement of more than a million? That remains an open question.

The question becomes even more pressing when we contemplate those home-schoolers who combine theologically inspired closed-mindedness with the desire to transform the nation as a whole in their own image. There is no way to know precisely how many families seek to inspire such ambitions in their children, though we have reason to hope it is relatively few. (With a student body of approximately 325 students, Patrick Henry is a very small college.) Yet apparently a great many of these relative few long passionately for political rule and have no interest in sharing it with their fellow citizens, many of whom they consider to be morally and religiously contemptible. Thanks to the irrepressible pluralism of modern America—not to mention our sometimes exaggerated fear of would-be tyrants—the effort of the most extreme evangelicals to gain and hold real political power will almost certainly fail. But that doesn't mean they won't make plenty of mischief along the way.

How, then, should the liberal political order respond to the challenge posed by evangelical home-schoolers? First of all, by acknowledging their right to educate their children as they see fit. However tempted we might be to judge as foolish the court rulings that have facilitated the exponential growth of the home-schooling movement, it is important to recognize that at the level of principle the cases were rightly decided. Just as liberalism demands that separatist groups within liberal society grant their members a right of exit, so it also demands that liberal society itself grant the same right to citizens who wish to exclude themselves from the education provided by the liberal state through the public schools. The principle isn't absolute. If the home-schooling movement continues to grow, and if significant numbers of its members continue to view their separatism as a prelude to overthrowing elements of the liberal political order, then the liberal state might have to revisit the issue in the name of defending the common good. But for now, Americans must learn to live with the reality of home-schooling and come up with a more creative response to the challenges it poses to the nation.[67]

In the end, the most productive approach might be a conciliatory one, acknowledging that home-schoolers sometimes have a point when they criticize the public schools. While the effort of the home-schooling movement to portray itself as a successor to the nation's parochial school system is unconvincing in many ways—Catholic private schools have usually seen themselves as vehicles of assimilation into the American mainstream for (often poor) Catholic immigrants, not as institutions designed to turn out doctrinally pure Catholics who would stand in opposition to modern American life—there is one respect in which the parallel between parochial schools and home-schooling is valid. The parochial school system was originally founded in response to blatant anti-Catholic bias in the public schools of the mid-nineteenth century. Rather than consigning the children of Catholic immigrants to a public school system that treated Catholicism as a backward religion that would have to be abandoned as a condition of participation in American democracy, the Catholic Church in America took it upon itself to create an educational alternative, one that would teach a more inclusive lesson. There can be little doubt that many of today's Christian home-schoolers see themselves in a similar light—as a beleaguered minority defending itself against a public school system fundamentally hostile to its deepest spiritual convictions.

For the most devout evangelicals, an antagonistic relationship with the public schools is probably inevitable. Such schools in an open society will never—and ought never—satisfy a Michael Farris, who in effect believes that all education must take the form of sectarian religious indoctrination. But what about those less rigidly pious? They, too, claim that the public schools are saturated with an ideological form of secularism that is openly and aggressively hostile to the traditional forms of belief they wish to pass along to their children. Though in some cases this might serve as an excuse to cover over other fears—of the crime, drugs, and premarital sex they believe infest the public schools—many traditionalists appear to be genuinely convinced that the public school system teaches ideas and attitudes that are fundamentally incompatible with their most deeply held religious convictions. This is an accusation that the public schools should take very seriously. When the public schools act as advocates for a comprehensive secular ideology that aims to stamp out all vestiges of traditionalist religion, they not only provoke dissenting families into dropping out of the public school system. They also commit an act of illiberalism.

A liberal society demands that its citizens tolerate differences, not that they approve of differences. It is a fine line, but a critically important one. Public schools should teach that all men and women have a nonnegotiable right to vote and participate fully in our political system, as well as the freedom to choose their own path in life without intimidation, the threat of violence, or other forms of coercion. At the same time, however, public schools must refrain from denouncing traditionalist beliefs about sexual and other matters as backward or rooted in ignorance or unthinking bigotry. Still less should they insist that the children of traditionalists positively affirm secular views of sexual morality and gender roles. To so do would be an example of the state illiberally using its power to stamp out differences in the name of respecting differences.[68] After all, a child of traditionalist Christians, Jews, or Muslims ceases to be a traditionalist the moment he or she is made to endorse behavior or beliefs that traditionalist Christianity, Judaism, or Islam explicitly holds to be wrong.

This is not to say that public schools should back down on fundamental matters of pedagogy. The bedrock of nonsectarian public education is and must remain the universally applicable scientific method of rigorously interrogating received truths. In fields where such investigation has yielded verifiable theories about the world, those theories must form the basis of classroom instruction. (Contrary to what some ill-informed creationists would like to believe, a scientific theory deserves to be treated as a fact unless and until it is proven wrong by contrary evidence.)[69] Given the indisputable evidence in favor of Darwinian evolution, for example, science classes must expose students to the findings of evolutionary biology. American history should likewise be taught using textbooks whose content is distilled from the work of professional historians, not from Christian apologists who rip statements of historical figures out of context in order to prove a polemical point about the fundamentally religious character of the nation. These matters are and must remain nonnegotiable.

But where no such scholarly or scientific unanimity exists—on matters of morals and metaphysics—the public schools should act with much greater caution, resisting the urge to inculcate any comprehensive ideology, including secularism. The most important—and universally applicable—lessons of liberal citizenship are minimalist ones that are best passed on to students tacitly, by encouraging them to investigate the world around them and to study, play, interact, and make friends with peers from different backgrounds, with differing views of the world. The role of teachers and administrators in this process of civic education is limited but vitally important: enforcing habits of inquisitiveness, toleration, and mutual respect among peers, and punishing acts of bullying and ostracism that are incompatible with them. A public school system that showed such restraint just might manage to halt the evangelical exodus out of the schools—and perhaps even encourage a handful of home-schoolers to return.

II

The Dangers
of Divine Authority

The word "religion" derives from the Latin "religio" (reverence for the gods) and "relegare" (constraint or obligation), and to this day members of various religious communities understand that their faith makes certain nonnegotiable demands on them—demands to which they are expected to submit, often without question. Some religious communities constrain more than others, and there is a wide range within Christianity. At one end, Unitarianism demands little to no obedience from believers. At the other extreme are those churches that emphasize the importance of submission to higher authority: evangelical Protestantism, orthodox Roman Catholicism, and Mormonism.

There are wide differences in how these three faiths conceive of ecclesiastical authority and its relationship to individual believers, but all of them demand obedience in some form. And that means that they teach something that stands in considerable tension with the public ethic of a liberal–democratic nation such as the United States. Whereas all three faith communities counsel submission to authority, liberalism insists on the distinction between legitimate and illegitimate forms of rule, with legitimacy determined (in large part) by whether or not a particular authority is willing to submit to the consent of the governed. The liberal order permits individuals to live partially in both worlds—to practice religious submission in the private sphere of life while upholding the principle of consent in political matters. Yet maintaining this distinction—keeping the opposing principles of authority consigned to their proper spheres—can be extremely tricky. Far from resembling a wall of absolute separation, the borderline between liberal and antiliberal notions of authority is constantly shifting as defenders of liberal politics and representatives of various traditionalist religions skirmish through history.

Sometimes it is traditionalist religion that finds itself on the defensive—as it did on March 5, 2009, when the Judiciary Committee of the Connecticut State Legislature introduced a bill into the General Assembly that proposed to strip legal, financial, and administrative control of every Roman Catholic parish in the state from church dioceses and give it to boards of directors comprised of between seven and thirteen lay people. If the bill became law, the pastor and bishop overseeing a given parish would continue to exercise power "in matters pertaining . . . to religious tenets and practices," but they would lose all control of the day-to-day functioning of the parish. The laity would in effect become employers of the clergy, thoroughly disrupting the lines of authority that normally prevail in the church as well as undermining and democratizing its hierarchical institutional structure.[1]

That the bill was tabled in a matter of days is probably for the best, since using the government to curtail church authority so dramatically would almost certainly have violated the First Amendment's protection of religious free exercise. Yet the issues raised in the dispute—authority, obedience, and submission—live on among

Catholics, evangelical Protestants, and Mormons. And in many cases what's at stake is not the freedom of religious groups to practice their faith without state interference but rather the very different but no less ominous problem of religious traditionalists pledging their allegiance to authorities that transcend and even conflict with the authority of the Constitution and the civic ideals that underlie it.

1

Throughout its history, evangelical Protestantism has combined democratic instincts with belief in the absolute authority of Scripture. Radicalizing the Reformation ideal of *sola scriptura* (by Scripture alone), American Protestants have tended to treat the Bible as the unmediated word of God, as the sole and transparently clear source of divine truth, and as absolutely binding on all Christians. Whereas in other cultural contexts such beliefs might have produced a class of authoritative scriptural interpreters, the egalitarian commitments of American evangelicals have led them in a very different direction—to the view that every man is empowered to serve as his own biblical exegete, provided that his interpretation is guided by his conscience and the ministrations of the Holy Spirit.

And yet, the demotic conviction that every individual is competent to assess God's intentions in the world has also, paradoxically, inspired a hunger for spiritual leadership—for a charismatic minister of Christ to distinguish himself from the crowd by proposing a uniquely insightful or emotionally powerful interpretation of the Christian mission. Such preachers can inspire remarkably intense devotion on the part of their followers, who understandably crave guidance in how to live in conformity with the word of the Lord as it is recorded in the Bible. In deferring to spiritual leadership, evangelicals often think of themselves as following the example of Christ, who likened himself to a shepherd caring for and lovingly leading his flock of sheep.

Social scientists have described this presumption in favor of hierarchy as "authority-mindedness."[2] Though it appears to arise from biblical assumptions and to be reinforced by habits of worship that emphasize the relationship between the pastor and his flock, it is by no means limited to church. On the contrary, evangelical culture is shot through with vertical social ties. In school, the teacher leads and pupils follow. At home, the mother defers to the father, while the children defer to the parents. At work, the employer rules and the employee defers. In each case, the figure in the position of authority receives deference, obedience, and the psychological rewards that flow from recognition of one's superiority, while those in the subordinate position enjoy love, care, and protection.[3] Ultimately, all of these hierarchical social connections are meant to model the most important relationship of all: the submission and humbling of the human will before the divine authority of a loving God.

As one might expect, the authority-mindedness of evangelicals bleeds over into politics. Sociologists John P. Bartkowski and Christopher G. Ellison have shown using public-opinion survey research, for example, that many evangelicals believe the ideal social order, like the ideal family, is "an organic whole" founded on "the biblical principles of authority and hierarchy"—one in which everyone fulfills a superordinate or subordinate role.[4] At the same time, many evangelicals also expect people to be led by sin (and especially the sin of pride) to rebel against these roles. Confronted by social conflict and disorder, a strong leader, like a strong father in the family, must therefore respond decisively, "often with physical force," in order to "shape the will" of transgressors.[5] Hence the tendency of evangelicals to spank or slap their children at noticeably higher rates than members of other groups in contemporary America.[6] Hence also their high levels of support for capital punishment—and even for the torture of terrorist suspects.[7]

More than other religious cohorts in modern American life, then, evangelical Protestants tend to believe in the importance of submitting to authority in private as well as public life. And yet we also know that evangelicals do not treat all authorities with the same degree of deference. In 1976, most evangelicals strongly backed the candidacy of Jimmy Carter. By 1980, many of them had become enthusiastic partisans of Ronald Reagan and the Republican Party. Over the next twenty-eight years, they mildly supported one president (George H. W. Bush), strongly supported another (George W. Bush), vociferously denounced and then robustly championed the impeachment of another (Bill Clinton), and passionately backed a controversial vice presidential candidate (Sarah Palin). (Preliminary data on white evangelical attitudes toward Barack Obama show considerable hostility.)[8] What accounts for the differences? Some of it surely flows from simple partisanship; for much of the past three decades, evangelicals have been, on the whole, loyal Republicans. But that doesn't explain the variation in evangelical support for Bush 41 on the one hand and Bush 43 and Palin on the other, let alone the intensity of evangelical enmity toward Bill Clinton, whose presidency was ideologically moderate in both domestic and foreign policy.

In order to make sense of these variations, we need to recall that evangelical views of obedience have their origins in the hunger for the spiritual leadership of a charismatic pastor or preacher. But the evangelical world is filled with potential shepherds looking to lead a flock of devoted Christians. How does an individual evangelical determine that a given preacher is a genuine minister of Jesus Christ and not a charlatan out to dupe believers for the sake of personal gain? Evangelicals have tended to make this determination on the basis of a judgment about the *sincerity* of the preacher's public testimony of faith. Has he been (or rather, does he claim to have been) born again in Christ? Does he appear to be animated by the Holy Spirit? Does he speak with passionate devotion to Jesus? Does he convincingly confess his sins to the community, begging humbly for forgiveness? The preacher who manages to persuade large numbers of Christians of the sincerity of his faith will inspire them to follow his leadership—to submit themselves freely to his authority.

The same dynamic comes into play when evangelicals vote, when they call the offices of their representatives in Washington, and when they answer pollsters' questions about their political opinions. In all these aspects of public engagement, evangelicals respond to what they take to be evidence of sincerity on the part of political leaders. Back in the early 1990s, for example, many evangelicals were inclined to support George H. W. Bush because they agreed with his policies and approved of his leadership during the Persian Gulf War. But when it came to public professions of faith, Bush was awkward and unconvincing, lurching between the cool, unemotional, understated style of mainline Protestantism—the very mode of worship against which evangelicals often see themselves in open, passionate rebellion—and inauthentic expressions of fervent piety. As a result, evangelical support for Bush during the crucial reelection battle of 1992 was solid but lukewarm.[9]

Bill Clinton, by contrast, spoke about his faith with what sounded like complete sincerity. And yet his behavior—from his seeming avoidance of the military draft during the 1960s to his later extramarital affairs—undercut his professions of faith in the eyes of many evangelicals, convincing them that Clinton cynically (and sinfully) deployed religion purely for the sake of political gain.[10] By the time the Monica Lewinsky scandal broke during Clinton's second term, evangelicals had grown thoroughly disgusted with the president. Convinced he was attempting to play them for suckers with his high-profile statements of anguished remorse, a majority of evangelicals concluded that Clinton deserved to be impeached and removed from office—showing that they were perfectly willing and even eager to challenge the authority of the nation's highest elected official once they believed he was guilty of serial insincerity.[11]

The equal and opposite dynamic could be seen at work in the presidency of George W. Bush—a politician who went out of his way to convince evangelicals that he both shared their religious convictions and planned to govern in a distinctively evangelical style. Bush spoke of his faith often and in a thoroughly evangelical idiom—emphasizing his sinful youth, his experience of being born again in Christ, and his confident certainty of the Lord's presence in his daily life. Evangelical identification with Bush increased even further after the terrorist attacks of September 11, 2001, which many traditionalist Protestants interpreted in providential and even eschatological terms, as a sign that the biblically foretold End Times were about to commence. The White House liaison to traditionalist Christians from 2001 until 2008, Timothy Goeglein, spoke for (and to) many evangelicals when shortly after 9/11 he told evangelical *World* magazine: "I think President Bush is God's man at this hour, and I say this with a great sense of humility."[12] Bush was the authoritative leader of the United States and the free world, due nearly absolute obedience; American citizens were called to follow him humbly, with utmost deference and respect.

Evangelical support for Bush thus began high and then dramatically increased during his first five years in office. Whereas Bush won 68 percent of the white evangelical vote in the disputed 2000 election, four years later the number had surged to 78 percent, the highest level of evangelical support on record for a general-election presidential candidate.[13] Moreover, having been persuaded that Bush was a born again follower of Christ sincerely seeking to do the Lord's bidding in the world, evangelicals remained extraordinarily loyal to him throughout his fraught second term. At the time of his second inauguration, 72 percent of white evangelicals approved of the president's job performance. Less than eighteen months later, in May 2006, Bush's support among this group of voters had fallen to 55 percent—but that was still significantly higher than his national job-approval rating, which by that point had sunk to 35 percent. These trends continued through the conclusion of Bush's presidency.[14] Many evangelicals apparently believed to the end that standing behind a divinely chosen leader through good times and bad was itself an expression of faith—faith in God, but also faith in providence, in having raised up a righteous man to lead the greatest nation on earth through uniquely challenging times.

The same evangelicals who considered Bush to be an agent of the divine apparently transferred their support to Sarah Palin once John McCain nominated her to be his vice presidential running mate in 2008. Palin, a longtime member of Pentecostal and evangelical churches, unapologetically described herself as a "Bible-believing Christian."[15] She argued that public schools should encourage sexual abstinence and foster the discussion of creationism. She denounced abortion as an "atrocity"—and silently demonstrated her integrity on the issue at the Republican convention by proudly displaying her five children, including her infant son Trig, whom she carried to term despite an in utero diagnosis of Down syndrome.[16] In return, evangelicals rallied to Palin's side, and they stayed there in the weeks leading up to the November election, as she repeatedly demonstrated her ignorance of the issues, and as the general population became understandably concerned about whether she possessed the knowledge and intelligence necessary to function as president of the United States.[17] To this day, white evangelicals remain the demographic group most likely to admire Palin and to pine for her to launch her own campaign for the White House.

The remarkable strength of evangelical faith, its persistence in the face of facts that disillusion less trusting citizens, its deference to political authorities who saturate their speeches with biblical platitudes, its hunger for easily forged expressions of spiritual authenticity—all of this is more than a little troubling. Liberalism permits citizens to affirm, espouse, adhere, and devote themselves to an enormous range of metaphysical views. But liberalism cannot and should not be indifferent to *how* those views are held, at least when they are brought into the political arena. Responsible self-government depends upon a citizenry habituated to respond skeptically, thoughtfully, and intelligently to the pronouncements of political authorities, just as it also requires that citizens place the good of the American people and their Constitution above personal attachment to any particular politician, no matter how effectively he or she affirms one group's parochial view of the world. This doesn't mean that liberal citizens must adopt a wholly critical view of political motivation, eschewing idealism, embracing cynicism, and automatically treating every politician with absolute suspicion. But it does mean that they need to recognize that good leadership and sincere leadership are not always synonymous. This lesson can be learned from passages of Scripture no less than from pages of history or stories on the nightly news. Either way, there is no excuse for allowing the longing for authority to become a justification of gullibility. Whether or not credulity is a theological virtue, it is undeniably a political vice.[18]

2

Attitudes toward authority among American Roman Catholics are even more conflicted than the ones that prevail among evangelicals. On the one hand, there appears to be very little that is distinctive about Catholic political opinions, which track very closely with those of the average American. George W. Bush won a slight majority (52 percent) of the Catholic vote in 2004, for example, while Barack Obama won a somewhat larger majority (54 percent) in 2008.[19] The Catholic embrace of the mainstream holds even when the church takes a firm stand on a particular issue, such as abortion. Although the Vatican condemns the practice and US bishops have recently started speaking out loudly against Catholic politicians who support a woman's constitutional right to terminate her pregnancy, individual Catholics are only slightly (five percentage points) more likely than non-Catholics to favor banning the procedure.[20] But perhaps no issue so strikingly captures the independent-mindedness of lay Catholics in the United States as the use of artificial birth control, which the church hierarchy explicitly condemns but which roughly 90 percent of American Catholics say they support.[21]

All of which might lead one to conclude that issues of authority and obedience are irrelevant to understanding the history and present reality of Catholicism in the United States. But that would be a mistake. Whatever the views of individual members of the American Catholic laity in the opening years of the twenty-first century, the institutional church has long made a series of claims that stand in stark contrast with the liberal view of authority. Not only does Catholicism have a long tradition of requiring submission to ecclesiastical rule (with bishops assumed to stand in direct succession from Jesus Christ and the original twelve apostles), but in the modern period leading Catholic theologians have developed an elaborate intellectual justification of the need for uncritical obedience to the authority of Rome. John Henry (Cardinal) Newman, for example, famously asserted that having "ten thousand difficulties" with the church's teachings on faith, morals, or doctrine ought not to "add up to a [single] doubt" about their truth.[22] A Catholic can have trouble affirming something taught by the Vatican, but in the end he must conclude that the difficulty arises from his own resistance to obedience or a misunderstanding, and not from any error in the teaching itself.

That is the theory. In practice, things have been, and remain, more complicated. Yet Catholicism's historic emphasis on obedience and deference to authority has placed it in frequent tension with American liberal–democratic habits and assumptions. Consider the 1888 statement of Pope Leo XIII: "The true liberty of human society does not consist in every man doing what he pleases." Rather, genuine liberty "supposes the necessity of obedience to some supreme and eternal law"—namely, to the divinely authored natural law proclaimed by the church. As historian John T. McGreevy points out, this vision of a necessarily symbiotic relationship between freedom and obedience—a vision of freedom as "ordered liberty"—stands in stark contrast to the prevailing liberal assumption that freedom consists in an individual's liberation from external constraints.[23] If the pope merely meant to say that, once granted political freedom, Catholics were obliged in their private lives to obey the moral and doctrinal strictures of orthodox Catholicism, the statement would be politically insignificant. But that is not—or not entirely—what he meant to say. On the contrary, Leo XIII was making an authoritative statement of the Catholic Church's fundamentally illiberal position on the proper ordering of human society as a whole, including the political sphere, in all times and places.

It was neither the first nor the last such statement. Throughout the late medieval and early modern periods, the Catholic Church conferred theological legitimacy on monarchical government, provided that the temporal authorities maintained Catholicism as an established church. The Vatican held to this position throughout the sixteenth, seventeenth, and eighteenth centuries, as it was placed on the defensive first by the Protestant Reformation, then by the critical spirit of the Enlightenment, and finally by the anticlerical violence of the French Revolution. By the early nineteenth century, the clerical hierarchy had decided actively to resist modern trends in politics, society, and culture, which it determined to be fundamentally antithetical to the interests and ideals of the church. In a series of strident encyclicals and other papal pronouncements issued throughout the nineteenth century—*Mirari Vos* (1832), the *Syllabus of Errors* (1864), *Longinqua Oceani* (1895)—the church positioned itself as the leading voice for political, social, and cultural reaction in continental Europe, unequivocally denouncing liberalism, religious freedom and toleration, democracy, pluralism, the separation of church and state, and religious "indifferentism" (agnosticism and atheism).

To many American ears, this sounded like a full-throated defense of tyranny. As long as the Catholic population in the United States remained small, few worried about the influence of such ideas on the country. But with the sharp rise of immigration from Catholic countries (especially Ireland) beginning in the 1840s, legitimate concerns about the church's hostility to liberal–democratic norms and ideals combined with cultural and religious xenophobia to create a noxious form of anti-Catholic prejudice. It was a prejudice indulged in by a wide swath of Americans, from members of local school boards to prominent writers and intellectuals such as William Ellery Channing, Horace Bushnell, George Cheever, and Theodore Parker. Parker spoke for many when in 1854 he denounced the Catholic Church for its fundamental hostility to liberalism:

> The Roman Catholic Church claims infallibility for itself, and denies spiritual freedom, liberty of mind or conscience, to its members. It is therefore the foe of all progress; it is deadly hostile to Democracy. She is the natural ally of tyrants and the irreconcilable enemy of freedom.

To his credit, Parker went on to admit that "individual Catholics" sometimes broke from the church in favoring the "progress of mankind." But these Catholics, alas, were "exceptional." The norm, according to Parker, was for Catholics—whether clergy or laity, whether in Rome or in the United States—to consistently hate "liberty in all of its forms," including "free thought" and "free speech."[24]

The reality, of course, was much less stark. Even before the founding of the first American diocese in 1789, the American church sought to establish some distance from Vatican rules and expectations— to show the predominantly Protestant population of the nascent United States that Catholics, too, could be good liberal citizens. The most successful such effort was the one begun by John Carroll in a series of meetings at Whitemarsh, Maryland, in 1783, 1786, and 1789, to establish a vibrant conciliar tradition of church governance in America. On fundamental matters of faith, morals, and canon law, the Vatican remained supreme. But when it came to less essential issues—how to respond to anti-Catholic currents in American culture, how to structure the rapidly expanding American parochial school system, how to meet the particular pastoral challenges faced by the church in the United States—the semi-regular convocation of the American clerical hierarchy at provincial councils, plenary councils, and diocesan synods throughout the nineteenth century proved to be extremely important. In the words of church historian Timothy M. Dolan, these meetings largely succeeded in providing "structure, organization, cohesion, and discipline to the internal life of the Catholic Church in America" while also showing the often anti-Catholic culture of the United States that the church was not "the backward, secretive, undemocratic, and foreign-controlled institution it was assumed to be."[25]

Unfortunately, however, the Vatican did not always approve of the relatively democratic habits practiced by the church in the United

States—especially when members of the church in the majority-Catholic countries of Europe showed signs of following the American lead. This is precisely what happened during the final decade of the nineteenth century. Following a recently translated hagiographical biography of American Catholic convert, priest, and founder of the Paulist religious order Isaac Hecker, some members of the French clergy took offense, claiming that Hecker had gone too far in adapting to the modern world by denying the objective truth of Catholic teachings and substituting an individualistic (and Protestant) emphasis on the primacy of conscience in moral deliberation.

Amplifying and intensifying these charges, Pope Leo XIII issued an apostolic letter in 1899 (*Testem Benevolentiae Nostrae*) that defined a new heresy called "Americanism." The document strongly implied that Catholics in the United States ran the risk of becoming heretics simply by accepting the legitimacy of key aspects of the nation's liberal political and social order: the separation of church and state, freedom of the press, and individualism. There could be no absolute freedom of thought or the press for Catholics, asserted the pope, because members of the church were duty-bound to submit themselves to the absolute authority of the hierarchy. They were duty-bound, in other words, unquestioningly to accept and affirm the Truth about faith and morals, and to reject moral and theological Error, as they were infallibly delineated by the church.[26] For members of the church in majority-Catholic countries, the document was just the latest in a long line of nineteenth-century pronouncements in favor of the political, social, and cultural rule of the Catholic clergy. For Catholics in the majority-Protestant United States, by contrast, the letter seemed to counsel withdrawal from political, social, and cultural engagement.

The American bishops, acutely embarrassed by the controversy over Americanism, promptly dismissed it as a "phantom heresy" and attempted to change the subject to other matters. Fortunately for them,

Pope Leo himself had recently proposed a different way for the church to conceive of its role in the modern political order. In the 1891 encyclical *Rerum Novarum*, the pope directed the church's attention to economics, highlighting the human suffering wrought by unrestrained capitalism while also rejecting communism as a viable alternative. In place of these illegitimate economic arrangements, Leo proposed a third way that mixed elements of each, affirming a right to private property but also supporting the right of the working class to form trade unions and engage in collective bargaining, and even endorsing laws mandating a living wage for workers.

While many European Catholics interpreted the document as providing theological support for the corporatist welfare state apparatus already established in Germany by Otto von Bismarck during the 1870s, American Catholics tended to come to a different conclusion. Immersed in a political system that up until that time provided little support for the poor, they read *Rerum Novarum* as a call to political engagement and reform. That placed the church firmly in the Progressive camp during the opening decades of the twentieth century. By 1919, the urge to contribute to the national movement for social justice had inspired the bishops to bring the American conciliar tradition to Washington DC in the form of the National Catholic Welfare Council (NCWC)—the church's first permanent bureaucracy in the nation's capital and the forerunner of the modern-day United States Conference of Catholic Bishops. Over the next two decades, the Catholic Church would become a potent political force, with the bishops speaking out through the NCWC in favor of "unions, government programs of relief, and . . . the National Industrial Recovery Act," and with Monsignor John A. Ryan coming to be viewed as the "unofficial chaplain of the New Deal."[27]

The roughly three decades separating the election of Franklin Delano Roosevelt and the convocation of the Second Vatican Council in

October 1962 marked a period of convergence between Catholicism
and American culture. Despite occasional outbreaks of anti-Catholic
prejudice—Paul Blanchard's 1949 book *American Freedom and Catholic Power* stands as a particularly egregious example—the trend during these years was toward the assimilation of Catholicism into the
mainstream, culminating in the election of John F. Kennedy, the
nation's first Catholic president, in 1960. The process of assimilation
ran in both directions. Not only did America's dominant Protestant
culture come, on the whole, to accept Catholicism, but the American
Catholic Church came to identify its public agenda almost entirely
with the New Deal liberalism of the Democratic Party. And so the old
nineteenth-century conflicts over authority and obedience within the
church and between the church and the modern liberal order faded
into irrelevance—a distant, unpleasant memory of little consequence
to the life of the nation or the lives of individual Catholics.

It is a considerable historical irony that the tension resurfaced in
the wake of Vatican II, the ecumenical council that sought, in part, to
open the church to the modern world. At the time Pope John XXIII
convened the council, the church officially held that the American norm of religious pluralism was merely a second-best political
arrangement to be permitted only where Catholics found themselves
in the minority. Where Catholics constituted a majority of a country's
population—in such European nations as Italy or France, for example, or in a United States of the future in which the demographic
situation had dramatically changed—an arrangement like the one
that prevailed in Francoist Spain, with Catholicism recognized and
protected by the state as well as controlling social policy, was clearly
preferable. The prelates gathered at the Vatican debated this position in a series of contentious meetings at the second, third, and
fourth sessions of the council, which stretched from April 1963 until
December 1965. In the end, the council approved a document (*Dig-*

nitatis Humanae), inspired (and largely written) by American Jesuit John Courtney Murray, that significantly reformed and liberalized the church's stance toward modern politics and society. That was a most welcome development. And yet the document also contained conceptual tensions—tensions deeply rooted in Murray's thought—that would lead to important (and disconcerting) real-world consequences over the subsequent decades.

In *Dignitatis Humanae,* the council sought to confer theological legitimacy on liberal–democratic government—a legitimacy the Vatican had always denied. To do so, participants endorsed a controversial argument that Murray had been making in his writings for many years.[28] In Murray's view, liberal ideals and institutions ultimately presupposed the dignity of the human person, and the dignity of the human person was ultimately grounded in Christian revelation.[29] From these axioms, it was but a small step to Murray's conclusion— namely, that a government committed to the protection of human rights is derived from and perfectly consonant with the revealed truth instantiated in natural law and proclaimed to the world by the Catholic Church. This was an extraordinary claim. After more than a century and a half of fundamental opposition to liberalism, the Vatican finally conceded its legitimacy. But the concession came at a price. The liberalism endorsed by the church had little to do with the history and theory of liberalism as it actually existed. It was a liberalism transformed, purified, sanctified—in a word, Catholicized.[30]

Predictably, the reality of life in liberal states since the end of Vatican II has clashed with the spiritualized vision of liberalism promulgated by the council. And that has created new versions of old Catholic problems with authority. Now, instead of issuing wholesale condemnations of liberal–democratic institutions and ideals, clerics and theologians engage in a high-minded form of partisan combat within liberal nations, issuing prophetic denunciations of mainstream policies for diverging from the Truth proclaimed by the church. Left-leaning Catholics chastise the political class for upholding free-market capitalism and fighting wars, while their counterparts on the right condemn sexual licentiousness and an insidious "culture of death" that supposedly preys on the most vulnerable members of society (the unborn and the elderly). In both cases, the nation is called to live up to its highest principles—with those principles understood in a distinctly Catholic light.

Religiously inspired social and political criticism can be perfectly legitimate and even admirable, of course. Yet there is something politically irresponsible about the post–Vatican II style of Catholic critique. In the debate about abortion, for example, the church's position goes far beyond demanding that individual Catholics refrain from terminating (or encouraging others to terminate) their pregnancies. The church insists that abortion should be outlawed, and that Catholic politicians must actively work to have it banned. If they don't, they risk public rebuke by outspoken priests and bishops and even face the possibility of having the sacrament of Holy Communion denied to them, as (pro-choice Catholic) Democrat John F. Kerry learned during his 2004 presidential campaign against (pro-life and non-Catholic) Republican George W. Bush.[31]

The problem with this position is not—or not primarily—that it seems to place the institutional church firmly on the side of one of the nation's two viable political parties—namely, the largely pro-life GOP. After all, the American hierarchy and laity sided even more unambiguously with the Democrats during the middle decades of the twentieth century. And besides, as Catholic supporters of a tough line on abortion often argue, it's not the church's fault that the Democratic Party decided during the 1970s to champion abortion rights, or that the Republican Party took a stand on the opposite side of the issue during this same period. If only both parties defended the rights and dignity of the unborn, there would be no reason for the church to single out Democrats for theological censure. But alas, the Democratic Party is overwhelmingly pro-choice, and that poses serious moral problems for Catholic Democrats seeking to remain in good standing with the church.[32]

This line of reasoning might be faulty. Perhaps a politician's stance on economic justice, war and peace, the death penalty, and other issues should be weighed equally with abortion when a church official decides whether he or she should be denied Communion. Or maybe priests and bishops—possessing no power to see into another person's soul, and sometimes guilty of their own sinful improprieties (sexual and otherwise)—have no business making judgments about whether an individual has committed a sin grave enough to justify the denial of a sacrament. Whatever the case, these are disputes internal to the church, with little political impact or implication.

Where the church's uncompromising position on abortion runs into political problems is in its demand, under threat of ecclesiastical penalty, that Catholic politicians oppose and work to deny the political freedom of female citizens to choose an abortion *despite the fact that the United States Supreme Court has declared it to be a constitutional right*. (That the Catholic Church forbids individual Catholics from choosing to procure abortions is, conversely, politically irrelevant. Like all private organizations, the church is perfectly within its rights in declaring what individuals must do to remain Catholics in good standing.) Members of the US House of Representatives and Senate swear an oath to "support and defend" the Constitution, just as the president swears to "preserve, protect, and defend" the same fundamental law. And yet, the Catholic Church in the United States (or at least an influential faction within it) would have Catholic congressmen, senators, and presidents contravene these oaths in the name of a higher authority—the authority of the vicar of Christ on earth, the Bishop of Rome—when the Vatican and the Constitution clash.

Five decades ago, John F. Kennedy sought to answer critics who worried that if he won the presidency he would confront a problem of divided loyalties—between his duty to uphold the Constitution and his duty to obey the Catholic Church's authoritative teachings on faith and morals. In his 1960 speech to the Greater Houston Ministerial Association, Kennedy responded by declaring that he believed in an America "where no Catholic prelate would tell the president (should he be a Catholic) how to act, where no public official either requests or accepts instructions on public policy from the pope, . . . [and] where no religious body seeks to impose its will directly or indirectly upon the general populace or the public acts of its officials."

It is not unusual today to hear Catholic intellectuals and members of the clergy denounce Kennedy's speech for its anemic view of Catholicism's role in American public life. The candidate inappropriately put his political ambitions ahead of his duty to the church, we are told, and dishonorably capitulated to anti-Catholic prejudice by declaring that Catholic politicians are required to suppress their religious convictions while in office. On the contrary, Kennedy's speech deserves to be recognized for its concise and eloquent expression of timeless political wisdom. Despite what certain roseate documents of Vatican II would have us believe, the liberal–democratic order of the United States is not perfectly harmonious with the moral teachings of the Catholic Church. There are, of course, some areas of overlap. But in other places they clash. And when they do—when the authority of the nation's fundamental law comes into conflict with the authority of the Vatican—it is the statesman's solemn duty to put the Constitution first.

3

Members of the Church of Jesus Christ of Latter-Day Saints (LDS, also known as the Mormons) face the prospect of similar clashes between their civic and spiritual duties. But the Mormon form of the dilemma is far more intense because it is wrapped up with a uniquely explosive concept of prophecy. Unlike the God of Protestants and Catholics—who is usually portrayed as the transcendent, all-powerful, all-good, all-wise creator of the temporal universe out of nothingness—the God of Mormonism is a finite God who evolved into His present state of divinity from a condition very much like our own and then merely organized preexisting matter in order to form the world.[33] Mormonism thus tacitly denies that the natural world possesses any intrinsic or God-given moral purpose. Everything we know—or could ever know—about right and wrong comes entirely from divine commands communicated to humanity by prophets. The idea of appealing to a higher principle against the word of a prophet—the idea, in other words, of using one's own mind to cast moral or intellectual doubt on the veracity of a prophetic pronouncement—makes no sense in the Mormon conceptual universe.

Intelligent commentators have always recognized that prophecy presents a potential challenge for earthly institutions, religious as well as political, since the prophet is the ultimate subversive, circumventing established lines of authority to receive revelatory wisdom and commands directly from the highest Authority of all. One approach to reining in prophetically inspired schismatic movements, which the Roman Catholic Church has refined over many centuries, is to rigorously distinguish between true and false, healthy and unhealthy forms of prophetic revelation—with the true and healthy defined as prophecy that is mediated by the institutional authority of the church hierarchy. A second approach, taken in varying ways by the dominant traditions of Judaism, Christianity, and Islam, is to claim that direct revelation ended in the distant past. Observant Jews tend to believe that revelation terminated with the death of the canonical prophets of the Hebrew Bible. Christians have identified numerous prophetic end points: the death of John the Baptist, the death of Jesus, the death of the last apostle, the Montanist crisis of the second century (when the prophet Montanus claimed revelations that superseded those of the apostles), and the closure of the New Testament canon.[34] And of course Muslims believe prophecy came to an end with the death of Mohammed.

The political response to the challenge of prophecy, at least in the centuries since the Protestant Reformation, has also tended to take two forms, both of which follow the lead of the churches in beginning from the presumption that the age of prophetic revelation is past. One tradition of thinking follows the suggestions of the seventeenth-century Thomas Hobbes, who developed a secular version of the Vatican's approach to prophecy, insisting that an absolute state should get to determine which, if any, prophetic claims will be considered genuine, with the good of the state sovereign serving as the only criterion of judgment.[35] To the present day, this remains the response to religion preferred by political authoritarians of nearly every stripe.

Then there is the liberal approach. The American constitutional framers preferred to rely on several informal social institutions that they hoped would diminish the likelihood that a self-declared prophet would gain enough followers to pose a threat to the authority of the liberal state. First, a vibrant commercial economy would moderate religious passions as individuals devote their lives to bettering their economic condition instead of seeking absolution for their sins. Second, the spread of scientific learning would inspire skepticism about claims to revelation, thereby shrinking the pool of those gullible

enough to believe in the veracity of one man's prophetic pronouncements. Finally, the founders hoped that by protecting and encouraging the "free exercise" of religion, the country's remaining faiths
would proliferate to such an extent that no single sect or group of
sects would be capable of attaining enough power to threaten the
political order of the nation as a whole. The framers believed, in other
words, that the political threat posed by prophetic revelation could be
mitigated by capitalism, science, and social pluralism.

They were too optimistic. In the half-century following the ratification of the Constitution, the new nation experienced series of spiritual
convulsions that historians have come to call the Second Great Awakening. Several existing denominations splintered during the period,
and many more were born, with a few of them claiming to have been
inspired by direct revelation. Shaker Ann Lee spoke of visions. Adventist Ellen White's transcriptions of her revelations fill several volumes.
But none of them matched the audacity of Mormonism's founder
Joseph Smith, a self-proclaimed prophet who brought forth entire new
works of scripture (*The Book of Mormon, Doctrine and Covenants,* and
The Pearl of Great Price) and even rewrote ("retranslated") passages of
the canonical Old and New Testaments in light of his personal revelations. But Smith not only founded the Mormon church on the basis of
his own prophetic utterances; he also transformed the mantle of the
prophet into an institutional office. To this day, the man who serves
as the president of the LDS church (along with his closest counselors) is considered a prophet—"the mouthpiece of God on earth,"
in the words of Mormon theologian and Apostle Bruce McConkie
—whose statements override mainstream Christian as well as previously accepted LDS scripture and tradition.[36]

Mormonism thus poses a distinctive set of problems and challenges for liberal–democratic politics. By elevating prophecy above
other sources of revealed truth and by insisting that the words of a

prophet supersede all Scripture and tradition, Mormonism opens the door to prophetically inspired acts and innovations, the content of which cannot be predetermined in any way—not to mention the possibility of a theologically grounded dictatorship of the Mormon prophet. Prominent Mormon (and future church president) Ezra Taft Benson indicated as much in 1980 with a famous statement of "Fourteen Fundamentals in Following the Prophet."[37] The prophet who leads the church, Benson claimed, "speaks for the Lord in *everything.*" Mormons can know that he will "*never* lead the church astray." Indeed, the prophet "can receive revelation on *any* matter, temporal or spiritual," including "civic matters," regardless of his education or field of expertise, because "the prophet is not required to have any particular earthly training or credentials to speak on *any* subject or act on *any* matter at *any* time."[38]

The exalted place of the prophet in Mormonism goes back to the church's founding by Joseph Smith. In the words of Smith's biographer Richard Lyman Bushman, Smith elevated himself and his prophecies above reason, Scripture, and experience. Those who listened to his revelations had to decide "to believe or not without reference to outside authority—common sense, science, the Bible, tradition, anything."[39] At the same time, Smith did not treat his own prophetic pronouncements as permanent statements of doctrine. On the contrary, Smith had "an aversion to creeds," believing that revelation "was forever evolving."[40] The prophet could thus overturn two-thousand-year-old scripturally recorded revelations in an instant, just as he could countermand his own previous revelations at a moment's notice. Compared with the extraordinary prophetic authority possessed by the leader of the Mormon church, the Roman Catholic pontiff, with his rarely invoked claim to infallibility in matters of faith and morals, is a modest ecclesiastical administrator.

Thoughtful Mormons are aware that the astonishing authority of the prophet is a potential problem, but the peculiarities of the church and its founding make devising a solution extremely difficult. One option would be for the LDS church to follow the lead of the Catholic Church in developing a tradition of philosophical reflection on natural law or some other moral ideal to which God and His prophets are assumed to be bound or co-equal. This rationalist tradition could then be used to check the veracity of prophetic pronouncements. The difficulty, however, is that Smith encouraged his followers to cultivate suspicion of philosophy unless radically limited by prophetic revelation. Mormons believe that Smith undertook a "great restoration" of authentic Christianity after an eighteen-hundred-year "apostasy" that began with the death of the apostles and the subsequent rationalizing of the faith that took place in the early church. According to Smith, it was questions like the one Socrates posed to Euthyphro—does God love what is good because it is good in itself, or is it good because God loves it?—that led the church fathers and early church councils into theological and doctrinal errors that corrupted Christianity for nearly eighteen centuries.

Some, however, have taken a different approach, insisting that Mormonism has no need of a binding moral theory because LDS revelation can and does check itself.[41] Smith did not limit prophecy to himself and his successors, but rather spread it widely throughout the church. Mormons inhabit a world as enchanted as the one described in the pages of the Bible, with prophets, seers, and revelators wandering the earth, speaking the word of God to the human race. In the words of Richard Bushman, "Joseph was designated as the Lord's prophet, and yet every man was to voice scripture, everyone to see God."[42] At the top of the hierarchy, the prophet shares his revelatory power with the two counselors who make up the First Presidency, while the remaining members of the Quorum of Twelve Apostles who lead the church also get to serve as conduits for revelation. But revelation doesn't stop there. Every adult male Mormon possesses "priesthood authority," making him the local arm of the "charismatic bureaucracy" that radiates out from Salt Lake City.[43] Each of these priests, as well as their wives, gets to stand before his congregation on Sunday morning to offer "testimony" of the experience of God in his life, of his personal revelation and confirmation of the divine truth as taught by the church. What Mormons mean when they claim that revelation can check itself is that somewhere along this line, members of the church would object to a spurious revelation emanating from the top.

Would they? Although revelation is spread widely throughout the church, Smith made it clear from the beginning that a divine experience at one level in the hierarchy can never regulate the authority of a higher level.[44] Authority flows down, not up. This was true at the time of the church's founding, when Smith condemned the rival revelations of church member Hiram Page.[45] And it remains true today, as Mormon Gail Turley Houston learned when she was denied tenure at church-run Brigham Young University for discussing her own heterodox (and feminist) revelations with students in class.[46] Prophetic revelations are perfectly acceptable, even encouraged, in Mormonism—but only if their content conforms to and reinforces the strictures established by the governing authorities.

A final group of Mormons have proposed that prophetic declarations can be checked by treating the currently accepted canon of scriptures revealed by Smith as the standard by which to assess all future revelations. In the words of Joseph Fielding Smith, the tenth president of the church, official LDS scriptural texts should be used as "the measuring yardsticks, or balances, by which we measure every man's doctrine."[47] This moderate and moderating view remains a controversial position in the church, however, and for good reason. None other than Joseph Smith and his successor prophet Brigham Young seemed to take a different stance toward the authority of revelation. Compared with "living oracles," Young declared, canonical works of scripture "are nothing," because they "do not convey the word of God direct to us now, as do the words of a Prophet or a man bearing the Holy Priesthood in our day and generation." To which Smith replied, "Brother Brigham has told you the word of the Lord, and he has told you the truth."[48]

There is thus no obvious way to rein in or limit the authority of the Mormon prophet–president—as became abundantly clear in the years following Smith's assassination in June 1844, when Young led his fellow Mormons on a migration to the American West to establish Zion on earth. Young allowed and encouraged his coreligionists to think of him as "God's representative in the flesh," as well as "our governor and our dictator," whose word was "sacred."[49] He accordingly ruled the Latter-Day Saints as a theocratic tyrant, enforcing a communistic system in which the church owned all the land in an area covering hundreds of thousands of square miles and graciously permitted families to live on and farm it, provided that they conformed to Young's edicts on (in his words) "everything connected with the building up of Zion, yes even to the ribbons the women wear."[50]

When members of the church failed to conform to Young's absolute rule, the consequences could be brutally harsh, thanks in part to the doctrine of "blood atonement." First promulgated by Young in 1849, the doctrine stated that in some cases Christ's atonement for humanity's sins needed to be supplemented by the actual shedding of the sinner's blood. By the time of the so-called Mormon reformation of 1856–58, this principle had become a justification for vigilante violence throughout the territories under Young's command, leading to numerous assaults on thieves, murderers, fornicators, adulterers, and apostates (usually called "covenant breakers"). The most horrifying of these vigilante attacks was undoubtedly the notorious

Mountain Meadows massacre of September 11, 1857, in which emi-
grants from an area of Arkansas known for anti-Mormon violence
were slaughtered by a Mormon militia as they passed through southern Utah on their way to California, leaving 120 men, women, and
children dead.[51] Whether or not Young explicitly ordered the assault
(the evidence is inconclusive), his doctrine of blood atonement clearly
deserves a fair share of the blame for creating an atmosphere in which
Mormons could believe that mass murder was demanded by God and
His prophet.

Since Brigham Young's death in 1877, the revelations of the LDS
Church's prophet–presidents have been less sensational—often using
radical theological means to achieve moderate political and social
ends. In 1890, for example, church president Wilford Woodruff published a prophetic manifesto that abolished the practice of polygamy,
thereby removing the primary obstacle to Utah's achieving statehood.
Likewise, on June 9, 1978, president Spencer W. Kimball announced
a revelation opening the Mormon priesthood to black members of the
church, implicitly conceding that previous church doctrine had been
infected by racism. In both cases, dramatic changes in Mormon doctrine were accepted with very little popular opposition, demonstrating the extraordinary power still wielded by Mormon institutional
authorities, who can fundamentally transform the religion with a
single pronouncement of revealed truth. At the same time, we should
recognize that far from posing a challenge to the liberal–democratic
order of the United States, both revelations brought the church into
much greater conformity with mainstream American values.

That tells us something important about the character of the Mormon church. Certainly Gordon B. Hinckley, who served as church
president from March 1995 until his death in January 2008 at the
age of ninety-seven, showed no sign of theological radicalism during his tenure as prophet. Indeed, as anyone who caught one of his

many jovial appearances on *Larry King Live* will attest, Hinckley was an exceedingly unthreatening figure. His successor as president, Thomas S. Monson, appears to be equally anodyne. In practice, the rigidly hierarchical structure of the LDS church is remarkably effective at enforcing conservatism. It is simply very difficult to rise to the top of the organization without being a consummate company man.

Yet the fact remains that, as it is currently constituted, Mormonism appears to lack the intellectual or spiritual resources to challenge a declaration of the prophet who runs the church with absolute authority, regardless of how theologically, morally, or politically radical that declaration might be. And with several Mormons expressing presidential ambitions, this should be cause for reflection, if not outright concern.[52] Members of the church may insist that non-Mormons have nothing to worry about, since God would never issue an immoral edict. But that is quite obviously a matter of faith—a faith that non-Mormons do not share. As long as the LDS Church continues to insist that its leader serves as a direct conduit from God—a God whose ways are, to a considerable extent, inscrutable to human reason—Mormonism will remain a theologically unstable, and thus politically perilous, religion.

III

The Folly
of Populist Piety

American universities and research institutes are the envy of the world, contributing in innumerable ways toward a wide range of scientific and technological projects: to lengthen the human life span, unlock the genome, cure diseases, store and transmit ever-greater quantities of information, uncover new and sustainable sources of energy, trace out the evolutionary history of life on earth, and even penetrate the mystery of existence itself through the study of cosmology and quantum physics. Yet the United States is also the know-nothing capital of the Western world. A scandalously large number of Americans apparently think, in blatant defiance of modern physics, astronomy, geology, and paleontology, that the world was created by God a few thousand years ago over the course of six days. An even larger number—in some surveys, well over 50 percent of the population—reject the most basic (and scientifically indisputable) elements of evolutionary biology. More troubling still, these beliefs are not limited to the population at large. On the contrary, as we have seen time and again in recent years, leading politicians and public figures often espouse them with pride, as proof of their populist bona fides. And then there are those who go even further, to treat ignorance itself as a sort of prerequisite for high political office.

While America's embrace of science and technology flows from the philosophical ideas of the Enlightenment, our suspicion of knowledge has its roots in biblical religion. According to one crucially important stream of theological reflection, sin and suffering enter into human life with the decision of Adam and Eve to disobey the divine prohibition against eating the fruit of the tree of knowledge. This view echoes throughout the Hebrew Bible and reaches a kind of climax in the chilling words of Ecclesiastes: "In much wisdom is much grief, and he that increaseth knowledge increaseth sorrow" (1:18). But no tradition has taken the injunction against the pursuit of knowledge to greater lengths than Christianity, which goes several steps beyond the Hebrew Bible to treat holy foolishness and childlike innocence as positive goods.[1] Christianity, it seems, turns the ideals of the Enlightenment on their head, teaching that knowledge leads to misery and estrangement from a God who prefers ignorance to wisdom about the ways of the world.[2]

At least in the abstract. In reality, Christianity has taken many positions on the worth of worldly knowledge. At one extreme of the Christian tradition stand St. Paul, the early church father Tertullian, and Protestant reformer Martin Luther, all of whom expressed intense hostility to reason and philosophy. At the other we find the highly developed tradition of Catholic theology stretching from Augustine through Thomas Aquinas and down to the present day. And then there is the wide range of attitudes toward independent thinking held by contemporary American Protestants. On one side are Episcopalians and other liberal denominations that permit their members to think, say, and write pretty much anything they wish. At the opposite end of the spectrum are a wide range of low-church Protestant groups, including Pentecostals, Seventh-Day Adventists, and Christian Scientists, not to mention thousands of churches of broadly evangelical orientation, whose members emphasize the importance of undergoing an experience of being born again, eagerly anticipate the imminent return of Christ, and forcefully reject key aspects of the scientific view of the world.

It is this last form of Christianity that lies behind much of the anti-intellectualism in contemporary American public life.[3] Why has the United States served as an incubator for a style of religiosity that treats science and scholarship with so much suspicion? It is a crucially important question, given the considerable intellectual demands of citizenship in a modern, liberal society. Although secular Americans sometimes treat the prevalence of religious belief in the United States as a danger to the liberal political order, religion in general isn't a problem. Obscurantist religion is. With its tendency toward anti-intellectualism, its heavy emphasis on emotionalism, its suspicion of skepticism, its impatience with complexity, its indifference to history, and its hostility to disagreement and dissent, the style of worship and belief that prevails among evangelicals, Pentecostals, and other low-church Protestants poses a unique set of challenges to the American political system.

Yet, if we wish to understand the precise nature of these challenges and devise appropriate responses to them, we must keep in mind that the anti-intellectual style of worship and belief is not some foreign contaminant that can simply be isolated and expunged from the nation, as some secular critics would seem to prefer. On the contrary, low-church Protestantism has been here, and flourished here, from the beginning. That raises an intriguing possibility—namely, that

America's own political culture might be in some sense the source
of or inspiration behind the very form of religion that clashes most
disconcertingly with political liberalism in the contemporary United
States.

1

Everybody knows that the Declaration of Independence contains
a bold and eloquent defense of human equality: "All men are created equal." With this simple phrase, Thomas Jefferson undercut
the assumption on which all hierarchical forms of government up
to that time had been based: that one person or class or group or
family or region can be entitled by nature or custom to rule over
others. According to Jefferson and the other fifty-five signatories of
the Declaration, the natural equality of all human beings implies
that political authority must be based on the consent of the governed in order to be rendered legitimate. When the people cease to
consent, the government becomes illegitimate and the people may
justly alter or abolish it, establishing a new government on properly
consensual foundations.

This is the radical idea that underlies liberal–democratic government in the United States and around the world. But the revolutionary character of the Declaration goes beyond its explicit endorsement
of human equality. Much of the document's rhetorical power follows
from Jefferson's decision to assert that this innate equality, like the
inalienable rights to life, liberty, and the pursuit of happiness with
which mankind has been endowed by its creator, is "self-evident." It
is obvious, an indisputable fact about the world—one that requires no
argument to understand, establish, or defend.

It would be difficult to exaggerate the subversive effect of Jefferson's public appeal to self-evidence in political affairs. All of us rec-

ognize that some people possess knowledge and expertise that others lack; this is why we seek out a medically trained surgeon to perform an operation instead of submitting ourselves to treatment by family members, neighbors, or fellow citizens who lack such training. Knowledge and expertise thus produce and perpetuate hierarchical social distinctions: the surgeon *deserves* deference on medical matters because he *knows more* about medicine than the rest of us. But what about politics? The presumption that some people exhibit more political wisdom than others famously led Plato to denigrate democracy and propose that the best form of government would be one in which philosophers rule: the wise man *deserves* deference on political matters because he *knows more* about statesmanship than the rest of us. In this way, the claim to knowledge contains within it an implicit claim to rule.

The appeal to self-evident political truths on the part of Jefferson and the other American revolutionaries fundamentally undermined the legitimacy of those who would justify their rule on the basis of knowledge or wisdom. This is because in a world of self-evident political truths, there is, strictly speaking, no such thing as politically relevant knowledge or wisdom. Sure, someone might possess political expertise about this or that subject, but *expertise does not necessarily entitle that person to political rule over his fellow citizens*. The decision about whether or not to bestow (temporary) political authority on this or that expert will be decided by the citizenry at large—by those lacking in any particular political knowledge or wisdom—through democratic election and other forms of political representation. It is therefore they—the nonexperts—who truly rule, and who truly *deserve* to rule, in a liberal democracy, because they have the capacity to perceive the self-evident fact of human equality. At the same time, the few who would deny this fact automatically disqualify themselves from rule by showing that their most elementary political perceptions are defective (perhaps due to ill-founded aristocratic or monarchical prejudices).

The Declaration's reference to self-evident truths—along with Thomas Paine's influential description of the insurrection against Great Britain as a matter of "common sense," which reinforced and even amplified Jefferson's egalitarian message—played an important part in the democratization of American political culture in the decades following the Revolution.[4] But these same ideas also left a decisive mark on the character of American religion. Just as knowledge or expertise can be used to justify a claim to political rule, so clerics have often asserted that their possession of esoteric knowledge, including the power to perform sacraments necessary for salvation, gives them authority within the church, and perhaps outside it as well. This dynamic was never as significant in the United States as it had been in Europe. The dissenting Protestants who settled New England in the early seventeenth century and did so much to set the religious tone in colonial America had rejected the notions of clerical privilege that prevailed in the rigidly hierarchical Roman Catholic Church and Church of England. In their place, the Puritans adopted a more egalitarian, congregational form of church organization. The elements of institutional hierarchy that remained were then dealt a further blow by the Great Awakening of the 1730s and 1740s, when charismatic preacher George Whitefield traveled throughout the colonies, spreading the gospel in a series of passionate revival meetings to enormous crowds of common people, urging them to undergo a heartfelt conversion to a life of devotion to God. It was the first stirrings of a distinctively American, radically egalitarian form of evangelical Christianity: popular preaching explicitly intended to evoke an emotional response.[5]

Still, Whitefield's preaching tour only hinted at what would follow in the early decades of the nineteenth century, when Protestant piety

decisively fused with democratic ideals, sparking the Second Great
Awakening. As historian Nathan O. Hatch has written, the popular
preachers of the time, who contributed to the founding or revival of
a slew of Protestant denominations (including the Baptists, Methodists, and Disciples of Christ), were "short on social graces, family connections, and literary education," and they "pitched their messages to
the unschooled and the unsophisticated."[6] Those who were swept up
into the revivalist spirit shared the belief in equality, denying "the age-
old distinction that set the clergy apart as a separate order of men"
and refusing "to defer to learned theologians and traditional orthodoxies." The result was an emotionally intense form of piety in which
preachers "openly fanned the flames of religious ecstasy," transport-
ing individual believers "beyond any doubts or fears or thoughts of
being . . . deceived." These populist ministers showed little interest in
subjecting such experiences to the "scrutiny of orthodox doctrine and
the frowns of respectable clergymen," let alone the "supposed lessons of history and tradition."[7] Each individual was promised a direct
encounter with Christ, unmediated by any established church hierarchy, authority, or institution. The preacher's role was to facilitate
this immediate divine experience—to give average people "a sense of
personal access to knowledge, truth, and power"—and not to control,
limit, or moderate it in any way.[8]

The populist preachers who led these revivals, no less than those
who participated in them, understood their intense spiritual experiences in part through the democratic rhetoric and ideas of the American Revolution.[9] Their encounter with Christ was, in their view, an
indisputable fact—a self-evident truth about themselves, the world,
and God, and one that was in perfect harmony with the common
sense of mankind.[10] As the century wore on, these elementary theological convictions linked up with and were reinforced by broader
trends in the culture. To be a Protestant in mid-nineteenth-century

America was in most cases implicitly to affirm a view of knowledge derived equally from the Scottish tradition of Common Sense
philosophy—which asserted that commonly held opinions are our
most trustworthy guide to truth—and (a naively simplified version
of) Francis Bacon's scientific method.[11] In the words of historian
George Marsden, nineteenth-century Protestants tended to assume
that "truth was a stable entity," that "basic truths are much the same
in all times and places," and that "in essentials the common sense of
mankind could be relied upon" as a source of knowledge, wisdom,
and understanding, whether about the ways of the world, the meaning of Scripture, or the veracity of personal revelations.[12] To achieve
scientific knowledge, one need only open one's eyes to passively perceive and record unbiased facts and then arrange them into precisely
stated propositions that can be conveyed, understood, and affirmed
universally.

It was a vision of intellectuality perfectly suited to a nation committed to the ideal of equality. Unfortunately, it also suffered from severe
conceptual difficulties, the most fateful of which was the weakness of
its account of disagreement. After all, if truth is the same everywhere
and always, and if it's equally accessible to all human beings via common sense, then it seems that all human beings ought to agree about
everything under the sun. But of course, they don't. What is the source
or cause of the divergence of opinion? For nineteenth-century Protestants, it was most likely some specific defect in the mind or morals
of whomever dissented from prevailing religious, scientific, social,
cultural, or political opinion. Maybe the dissenter had succumbed
to the sin of pride, which led him astray. Or perhaps he made an
innocent error of reasoning, or got caught up in futile metaphysical
speculation. And then there was the most ominous possibility—that
he was seduced by unbelief or false religion.[13] Whatever the case, the
disagreement was assumed to flow not from the intrinsic complex-

ity of either the world or the nature of the mind but rather from an accidental failing rooted in a particular individual or group—a defect that could potentially be removed, thus restoring the inevitability of universal agreement based on self-evident common sense.[14]

2

This was the peculiar dogmatism of American Protestantism in the nineteenth century. Unlike, say, the dogmas of the Catholic Church, which are specific articles of faith and morals that the church hierarchy declares on the basis of its own authority and tradition to be binding on Catholics, American Protestant dogma promised spontaneous universal concord among all human beings on every matter of moral, scientific, and spiritual significance. Men and women need only open their eyes to apprehend directly the timeless, objective, self-evident truth about all things: God, nature, right and wrong.[15] The very idea of a genuine (as opposed to a spurious) conflict between reason and faith, science and religion, was inconceivable, as was the idea that knowledge could produce or justify hierarchical social distinctions. Knowledge, after all, was equally accessible to all and perfectly compatible with—perhaps even synonymous with—the common sense possessed by everyone. As long as the findings of science did not directly challenge claims to revealed truth and a rough consensus on moral and religious matters prevailed in the churches and in American society, the hope for universal egalitarian harmony contained within Protestant dogma maintained its plausibility. When conflict broke out on multiple fronts in the opening decades of the twentieth century, those hopes quickly crumbled.

The demotic evangelical spirit unleashed during the Second Great Awakening burned throughout the nineteenth century, as denominations, and congregations within denominations, competed with one another for members in the spiritual marketplace opened up by the First Amendment's guarantee of religious "free exercise." New sects were formed, older ones broke apart, and religious entrepreneurs such as Dwight L. Moody built revivalist networks of churches, seminaries, and Bible institutes to train armies of ministers and missionaries who were sent forth to proclaim the gospel throughout the country and the world.[16]

In this spiritual hothouse, radical new ideas and practices continually flared up and died out. A few persisted, drawing on older democratic convictions and helping to form the sensibility of evangelical Protestantism as it confronted unprecedented challenges in the opening decades of the twentieth century. One of these ideas was the notion that God relates to human beings in different ways during distinct historical epochs or "dispensations." Brought to the United States in the mid-nineteenth century by John Nelson Darby, an early leader of the Plymouth Brethren, the outlook quickly fueled eschatological hopes and fears, convincing many that the End Times described in the Bible were imminent—and that it was possible to search for evidence of God's intentions by interpreting history and current events in the light of the most elaborately allegorical passages of the book of Revelation. Those who affirmed this view, called "premillennial dispensationalism," tended to believe that a faithful, common-sense reading of Scripture could provide certain guidance to ordinary Christians as the world entered an epoch in which the forces of good and evil, God and Satan, would wage their final, apocalyptic battle.[17]

In its emphasis on using the Bible as an all-purpose, unmediated guide to life in treacherous times, premillennial dispensationalism grew out of and reinforced another late-nineteenth-century trend in American Protestantism: the belief in biblical inerrancy. First proposed in an 1881 book by a pair of American Presbyterian theologians

from Princeton Seminary, Archibald Alexander Hodge and B. B. War-
field, the notion that every passage of the Bible is literally true and its
meaning transparently obvious to anyone at any time or place who
reads it faithfully fired the imaginations of evangelical Christians,
building as it did on old American assumptions about the ahistorical,
common-sense character of truth. In the words of Archibald Hodge's
father, Charles Hodge (another Princeton theologian), "the Bible is to
the theologian what nature is to the man"—namely, a "store-house of
facts" waiting to be compiled into truthful, scientifically valid propositions.[18] The Christian's duty is simply to collect the "wholly accurate
facts" provided by God and then apply them directly to his life, just as
the scientist (according to the naive Baconianism of the time) orders
the facts derived from observation of the natural world into universal
knowledge.[19]

But the most significant late-nineteenth-century theological development was undoubtedly the rise of Pentecostalism, an astonishingly
energetic grassroots movement that pushed the egalitarian individualism and ecstatic immediacy promised by earlier revivals further
than ever before, teaching that it was possible for average Americans,
regardless of background or education, to undergo an intense personal encounter with the person of the Holy Spirit. Pentecostalism
arose from two separate but compatible theological traditions—one
of them the "Holiness" branch of Methodism, the other a "Baptis-
tic" or "Keswick" form of worship that grew out of the Reformed
churches—both of which stressed "salvation in Christ, divine healing, the baptism of the Holy Spirit (eventually thought to be manifest
most clearly through speaking in tongues), and the imminent return
of Christ."[20] The two traditions also followed the lead of Pentecostal
leader A. J. Tomlinson in treating it as a point of pride that the new
style of worship and belief involved "no creeds, rituals, or articles of
faith," relying instead on "the Bible for everything."[21] In the years

following its full emergence at the 1906 Azusa Street revival in Los Angeles, Pentecostalism spread rapidly throughout the country and eventually the world. Today Pentecostal churches claim 250 million members worldwide, but it is a radically decentralized faith, splintered into roughly three hundred denominational variations in the United States alone. What they share is the radically egalitarian ambition to make "meaning for this world and salvation for the next . . . available to everyone, however ignoble."[22]

For those swept up in these overlapping demotic movements within American Protestantism, the opening decades of the twentieth century were a deeply disquieting time. The nation's cities were filled with impoverished immigrants, many of them from non-Protestant (and in the case of Jews, non-Christian) cultures. At the same time, industrialization was transforming American life in unpredictable ways, disrupting small-town life, driving the young to seek their fortunes in those same cities, exposing them to unimaginable moral temptations and objectionable ideas. Meanwhile, the nation's public schools were beginning to introduce Christian children to disturbing new unbiblical theories about the origins of the human race. For a Pentecostal or an evangelical Protestant inclined toward a belief in biblical inerrancy or premillennial dispensationalism, the suggestion that human beings evolved from apes sounded both morally monstrous and fundamentally unscientific—a form of demonic speculation wholly divorced from a properly common-sensical study of the natural facts.

Perhaps most disconcerting of all was the rise of theological liberalism—or "modernism"—in some of the nation's leading churches.[23] Instead of responding to these disturbing modern trends as traditionalist Christians—by, say, calling on believers to reaffirm established moral and religious views—the modernists accepted the legitimacy of many of these same trends, including biblical criticism and archeological research that cast doubts on the literal truth of Scripture. Liberal theologians and social activists such as Richard T. Ely, Washington Gladden, Walter Rauschenbusch, and Charles Sheldon were inclined to treat the Bible as a compendium of religious experiences and moral teachings whose literal veracity was beside the point. The importance and significance of the stories recorded in Scripture lay in their ability to inspire human beings in the here and now to transform the world as fully as possible into the kingdom of God on earth.

As far as more traditionalist Protestants were concerned, the spread of such ideas within the nation's churches and seminaries was a deeply distressing, even cataclysmic, development. Lacking the intellectual resources to make sense of serious theological disagreement and disinclined to accept the scientific findings that inspired liberal dissent in the first place, many traditionalists chose the retrenchment of fundamentalism. Consumed with dread at the fracturing of American Christianity, they demonized their liberal opponents, failed to engage with their arguments, and dismissed the scientific discoveries that led many Christians to doubt numerous elements of traditional Christian belief. In place of doubt, the traditionalists put willful certainty, declaring that their religious convictions were true despite their incompatibility with the findings of modern science. Going even further, they drew on deep-seated democratic convictions to insist that because their traditionalist views comported with the common-sense beliefs of average (often uneducated) Americans, those views expressed scientific truth.

3

Acclaimed Notre Dame historian Mark A. Noll, himself a devout evangelical, has written the most poignant critical examination of such assumptions, showing that serious intellectual engagement largely

died out in the evangelical community with the rise of fundamentalism in the 1920s. From that point forward, evangelical thinking
would be marked by a pronounced lack of "self-criticism, intellectual
subtlety, or an awareness of complexity."[24] It would treat oversimpli-
fication as an intellectual virtue and eagerly substitute "inspiration
and zeal for critical analysis and serious reflection."[25] Rejecting out
of hand the learned opinion of those (scientists and scholars) who
devote their lives to studying the world and humanity, hostile to exam-
ining the "forces in history that shape perceptions and help define the
issues that loom as most important to any particular age," evangelicals have turned inward, relying on nothing outside of the Bible and
their own unexamined theological convictions to make sweeping, ill-
informed pronouncements about "God, the human condition, [and]
the fate of the world."[26] No wonder, then, that in the eighty or so years
since the evangelical community gave birth to fundamentalism, it has
produced "no fundamentalist philosophy, no fundamentalist history
of science, no fundamentalist aesthetics, no fundamentalist history,
no fundamentalist novels or poetry, no fundamentalist jurisprudence,
no fundamentalist literary criticism, no fundamentalist sociology."[27]
Fundamentalism, according to Noll, has been an unmitigated intellectual disaster for evangelical Protestantism in the United States.

That this has been its fate is all the more surprising because it
began with some intellectual promise. Troubled by trends in the
country and the churches, a group of pastors and theologians set out
to distill the essence of traditionalist Christianity in the pages of a
book that could be distributed free of charge to ministers and missionaries around the country. Financed by businessman Lyman Stew-
art, published by the Bible Institute of Los Angeles between 1910 and
1915, and eventually containing ninety articles in twelve paperback
volumes, *The Fundamentals: A Testimony to the Truth* was meant to
serve as an intellectually respectable bulwark against liberal theology

and other modern trends.[28] In a sign of the book's unremarkable content, many in the secular press (including the editors of the *Nation* and the *New Republic*) took the side of the fundamentalists, conceding that they had a point in criticizing theological modernists for using traditional Christian terminology to describe profoundly unconventional political, moral, and religious ideas.[29]

And yet, *The Fundamentals* also contained the seeds of the more radical position that would soon bloom among the traditionalists.[30] On page after page, the book's contributors assumed not only that a literalistic reading of Scripture was perfectly *compatible* with science, but also that the findings of science would *reinforce* traditionalist biblical teachings and common-sense moral beliefs. This longstanding evangelical Protestant conviction could be maintained with relative ease in the early decades of the nineteenth century. But by the early decades of the twentieth, the widespread acceptance of Darwinian ideas in educated circles had raised the frightening possibility that science might veer off in explicitly unbiblical directions. Rather than update their understanding of the Bible in the light of scientific discoveries, as their modernist opponents had already done—and instead of proudly proclaiming their wholesale rejection of science and explicitly embracing holy ignorance—the fundamentalists set out on a more muddled (and intellectually disastrous) path. In the years following the publication of *The Fundamentals*, traditionalist evangelicals began to assert that a naively literalistic reading of the Bible teaches "true" science, and that when practicing scientists diverge from these biblical truths their findings are self-evidently unscientific.

This claim began to be made in earnest between 1917 and 1920, as the traditionalists reacted to the latest provocations of the theological modernists, who were growing increasingly radical in response to the destabilizing social traumas of the First World War.[31] By the mid-1920s, the clash between conflicting visions of science—one the form of inquiry practiced by actual scientists, the other a consoling construct of the evangelical imagination—was being played out around the country. Inspired by fundamentalism's confident defense of literalistic biblical truth, states had begun to pass laws prohibiting the teaching of evolution in public schools. In 1925, a Tennessee high school teacher named John Scopes was charged with violating the state's Butler Act, which banned the teaching "of any theory that denies the Story of Divine Creation of Man as taught in the Bible, and to teach instead that man has descended from a lower order of animal."[32]

In making the case for the prosecution in what has come to be known as the Scopes "Monkey" Trial, evangelical William Jennings Bryan expressed the new fundamentalist consensus with admirable concision, asserting that the truths conveyed by the Bible and common sense are identical with the findings of science, rightly understood. "It is not scientific truth to which Christians object," Bryan insisted, but merely to demonstrably false claims to scientific truth. And how can a Christian determine if a scientific finding is true or false? By looking to the Bible, which sets the standard for all knowledge. On the matter of evolution, for example, the story of creation from the book of Genesis demonstrates beyond a shadow of a doubt that "evolution is not truth" but merely a "hypothesis"—and an exceedingly tenuous one at that, consisting as it does of nothing more than "millions of guesses strung together."[33] This is why, according to Bryan, it was perfectly reasonable for the Christian citizens of Tennessee to insist that public school science classes exclude the idle speculations of evolutionary biologists and actively inculcate the ironclad truths of biblical creationism in their place.[34]

The jury was persuaded. Yet fundamentalism's minor victory in Tennessee did not inspire traditionalists to continue their crusade against theological modernism—at least not right away. Although the verdict was soon overturned on a technicality and never appealed, Bryan's passionate defense of traditionalist evangelical beliefs had been harshly ridiculed in court by defense attorney Clarence Darrow, whose criticisms were then loudly amplified in newspaper coverage of the trial, humiliating and demoralizing traditionalist Protestants around the country. Over the next few years, support for fundamentalism would wane in parishes and seminaries where it had briefly seemed to be on the brink of spearheading a successful purge of theological modernists. It would take nearly four decades for evangelical fundamentalism to reassert itself culturally and politically. When it did, its champions would employ new, more sophisticated arguments and strategies of persuasion. But its underlying assumptions—about the possibility of using the Bible as a guide to understanding the natural world, about the self-evident, common-sensical character of truth, and, most of all, about the importance of using Scripture to distinguish between true and false forms of science—would be precisely the same.

4

The resurgence of evangelical fundamentalism during the second half of the twentieth century was inspired in large part by the rise of "scientific" creationism. Prior to the 1930s, most evangelicals (including literalists such as William Jennings Bryan) assumed that the earth was many thousands, if not millions, of years old. The idea that the Bible could be used to establish the precise age of the planet—and that the earth was considerably younger than previously believed—can be traced back to the speculative writings of Ellen G. White, the founder of Seventh-Day Adventism, and her theological descendant Adventist George McCready Price, who wrote the founding text of modern creationism, *The New Geology*

(1923), which argued that a simple reading of early Genesis showed that God had created the world a few thousand years ago and had used the Flood to construct the planet's geological past.[35] In Price's view, the surest way to attain a scientific understanding of the earth's geology—certainly a much surer way than studying it in the way a modern geologist would—was to read the Bible as literally and uncritically as possible.

Price's remarkable claims at first exercised minimal influence on evangelical culture. Only in 1961, when John C. Whitcomb, Jr., and Henry M. Morris updated Price's work in *The Genesis Flood*, did large numbers of evangelicals begin to embrace and espouse creationist ideas. Not only did Whitcomb and Morris promise to protect the biblical status of humans as uniquely created in God's image, they also suggested it was possible to do so in rigorously scientific terms. That led evangelicals, once again, to imagine that science exists in two forms: one wicked, the other righteous. The first, satanic form of science is espoused by the country's intellectual establishment; it teaches that the earth is 4.6 billion years old, that evolution operates according to a process of random mutation and natural selection that produces frequent mass extinctions, and that humans evolved from lower life-forms. The second, biblically derived form of science teaches that the earth is roughly 6,000 to 10,000 years old, that all species were created simultaneously, and that mass extinctions took place at the same time in the past and were caused by a cataclysmic worldwide flood. Which form of science is true and therefore scientifically valid? The second, of course—but not because those who practice it have compiled more compelling empirical evidence in its favor. Rather, the second form of science is true and therefore scientifically valid because it alone begins and ends where all truth must begin and end: with the God revealed in the Bible and in the common-sense religious experiences of believers.[36]

So-called scientific creationism flourished in the evangelical community during the late 1960s and 1970s, contributing to the most powerful revival of fundamentalist enthusiasm since the 1920s and inspiring traditionalists to push back against court rulings (the most important of which was *Epperson v. Arkansas*, upheld by the US Supreme Court in 1968) that had overturned on First Amendment grounds the nation's many state-level anti-evolution statutes. By the 1980s, this energy had been channeled into the political arena by grassroots organizations such as Jerry Falwell's Moral Majority, which worked to bring selected states back into line with evangelical assumptions. In 1981, for example, the Arkansas legislature passed a bill granting "equal time" in public schools for "evolution science" and "creation science." Louisiana's "creationism act" likewise mandated that "creation science" be paired with evolution in the state's science curriculum.

Federal courts have repeatedly struck down these and similar laws.[37] These setbacks, in turn, have prompted evangelicals to try two new tactics in their bid to get scientific creationism taught in the public schools. The first has been to pressure publishers into pasting stickers on biology textbooks, declaring that "evolution is a theory, not a fact, regarding the origin of living things."[38] As many critics have noted, the statement—which is clearly intended to sow skepticism about evolution in the minds of children—is at best trivially true and at worst blatantly misleading. Contrary to what fundamentalist evangelicals might believe, science is not done by compiling self-evident facts about the world and then restating them as simple propositions. Rather, science constructs theories to explain facts, seeks out evidence to confirm the theories, and remains open to the discovery of new factual evidence that would falsify them. If evolution is "a theory, not a fact," then so is general relativity, quantum mechanics, and every other scientific account of nature. At the same time, however, it is perfectly reasonable for a layman to speak of reigning scientific theories as "facts" about the world, since they represent humanity's best attempts to explain that world—attempts that deserve to be considered true, at least until they are falsified by contrary evidence at some point in the future. Scientist Jerry Coyne is thus surely right to remark that, in light of the overwhelming evidence confirming evolutionary biology, "it makes as little sense to doubt the factuality of evolution as to doubt the factuality of gravity."[39]

The second tactic employed by fundamentalist evangelicals in recent years has been to develop yet another alternative form of science—one that aims to earn respect in the secular academy—called "intelligent design" (ID). ID goes beyond scientific creationism in two ways: it concedes some validity to evolution, and it raises empirically based objections to which evolutionary biologists can (in principle) respond. And yet, ID's leading lights have been perfectly clear that their project is ultimately motivated by the desire to defend traditionalist Protestantism against the advance of science. Evangelical mathematician and ID proponent William Dembski, for one, has written that he believes "God's glory is being robbed by . . . naturalistic approaches to biological evolution, creation, and the origin of the world."[40] Similarly, Phillip E. Johnson, an evangelical lawyer whose 1993 book *Darwin on Trial* advanced an early version of ID, has portrayed Darwinism as the latest in a line of now-discredited ideologies (including Marxism and Freudianism) that have sought to dethrone the Christian God in the name of science. To be truly open-minded, Johnson asserts, scientists would have to stop excluding evidence for divine creation from their work and realize how many problems in the standard evolutionary account would be solved by appeal to a cosmic designer of life.[41] Doing so would transform science as it is currently practiced into a form of inquiry that yields findings that confirm and conform to the theological truths gleaned from a literalistic reading of the Bible.

In its most simplistic version, ID highlights missing links in the fossil record between major forms of life—between, for example, early fishes and later amphibians or early reptiles and later mammals—and then proposes to find God in those "gaps" in the evolutionary account. (Hence the phrase "God in the gaps," which is how critics of ID have come to refer to its vision of divinity.) ID suggests, in other words, that evolutionary theory needs theology to complete its work because it is powerless to explain how one major form of life transforms into another—at least without reference to a designer who creates these major forms *ex nihilo*.

The problem with this approach is that it treats the currently imperfect state of the fossil record as if it gave us definitive and exhaustive information about the evolutionary history of life on earth: no transitional fossils, no transitional species. In fact, however, paleontologists are discovering new fossils all the time—and, indeed, have found fossils showing numerous transitional forms between major groups, and at precisely the right time in the fossil record, "after the ancestral forms already existed, but before the 'linked' later group had evolved."[42] The response of ID advocates to such discoveries has been what one would expect: they have fallen back to new positions, taking their stand on the remaining gaps in the fossil record, "continually retreating before the advance of science."[43]

Other proponents of ID have taken a more refined approach to challenging evolutionary theory. Starting in 1996 the Center for Science and Culture (CSC) at the Seattle-based Discovery Institute—which defines its mission as replacing "materialistic explanations with the theistic understanding that nature and human beings are created by God"—began to support the work of trained scientists who could make the argument against Darwinism with greater authority. The most formidable scholar associated with the CSC, biochemist Michael Behe, has developed and defended a unique line of argument against Darwinian evolution.[44] While Behe grants the explanatory power of Darwinian assumptions, he also claims that these assumptions leave enormous gaps in the evolutionary account. Behe makes his case by arguing that, although a process of environmental adaptation and random mutation can explain microevolution (small changes in a preexisting organ or system in a species), it cannot account for the origin of those organs or systems themselves, especially when they show signs of "irreducible complexity." The human eye, for example, depends on the precise interaction of dozens of parts, the removal of any one of which makes vision impossible. The same holds for the process of blood clotting, which requires the presence and complicated interaction of multiple proteins.

According to Behe, it is simply inconceivable that such complex systems—which function only when each and every component is present and performing a particular and necessary role in the process—could have arisen out of adaptation and random mutation. Such complex systems thus show signs of "intelligent design," just like any human invention (such as a wristwatch or a mousetrap) that requires the precise interaction of multiple parts. To hold otherwise is to maintain the far more fanciful view that one day millions of years ago a previously eyeless organism gave birth to a random mutation with precisely the right combination (and interaction) of parts to enable vision. Which explanation—the intervention of an intelligent designer or the random production of an irreducibly complex function out of thin air—sounds more sensible? That is the common-sense question posed by the most intellectually formidable and scientifically literate champion of ID.

Yet, as evangelicals have learned—or should have learned—at many points in their history, the comforting simplicities of common sense rarely comport with the far more intricate and often counterintuitive truths revealed by science. Common sense tells us, after all, that the sun circles the earth, rising in the east, traversing the sky, setting in the west, with the planet standing perfectly still beneath it. The truth—disclosed by scientific investigation, which subjects the common-sense experience of the world to systematic scrutiny—is of course very different. Something similar could be said of naively literalistic readings of Scripture or religious experiences that supposedly confirm those readings. Genuine science is and always will be the enemy of the credulity that makes it possible to believe in the veracity of such readings and experiences. And that is why each and every evangelical attempt to devise an alternative, faith-friendly form of science must end in delusion and obscurantism. Religious believers can reject science wholesale, or they can follow the lead of theological modernists and adopt a revisionist form of faith on the basis of scientific truth. What they cannot do is what evangelicals have repeatedly attempted and failed to do, which is to have it both ways.

That brings us back to the human eye and its supposed "irreducible complexity." As critics of Behe's work have argued on numerous occasions, what appears to be irreducibly complex can more accurately be described as the latest stage in a long process of refinement in a rudimentary but functional system, each stage of which improves on the one that preceded it. The most primitive eyes could detect little more than the difference between light and darkness. More evolved versions added simple lenses and then the capacity to focus, with the human eye found at the end of the adaptive process, its complexity perfectly "reducible" to what came before it. The evolutionary history behind blood clotting is more opaque, but we have reason to believe that there, too, scientists will eventually come to understand the evolution of the biochemical pathways that make it possible—that is, as

long as we continue to seek that understanding. In the words of evolutionary biologist Jerry Coyne,

> it is simply irrational to say that because we do not completely
> understand how biochemical pathways evolved, we should give
> up trying and invoke the intelligent designer. If the history of
> science shows us anything, it is that we get nowhere by labeling
> our ignorance "God."[45]

5

Democratic ideals can inspire intense hostility to intellectuality, especially when they fuse with a religious tradition already inclined to
look with suspicion on the life of the mind. That is one important
lesson to be learned from the career of evangelical Christianity in
the United States. Since the Second Great Awakening, if not before,
evangelicals have drawn on the egalitarian rhetoric and ideas contained in the nation's founding documents to make sense of their
spiritual lives. They have distrusted authority. They have placed their
faith in the common sense possessed by ordinary men and women.
They have assumed the self-evident truth of their personal religious
convictions. They have responded to populist appeals and embraced
revivalist styles of preaching and worship. They have craved immediate and ecstatic experiences of the divine. And they have reacted
with fear and hostility to those (especially natural scientists) who have
presumed to plunge beneath the consoling surface of life in order to
acquire religiously and morally unsettling knowledge about mankind
and the world.

The last of these poses the greatest challenge to liberal politics.
The challenge does not so much arise from evangelical misgivings

about science per se, since political liberalism is not committed to the truth of any particular scientific theory. Rather, evangelical misgivings about science tell us something important, and troubling, about the willingness of evangelicals to close their minds to reality the moment it begins to make things difficult for their faith. This is a problem for liberalism because openness to reality in all of its variousness, complication, and complexity is a crucially important component of liberal citizenship.[46] In their tendency to treat truth as something obvious, simple, and self-evident, in their sentimental veneration of common sense, in their indifference to exploring the humbling intricacies of history, in their absence of curiosity about other cultures and the workings of nature, in their propensity to see disagreement as a sign of sinister motives rather than a product of the multifaceted character of human experience, in their refusal to restrain their egalitarian commitments even when they threaten to undermine the pursuit of knowledge about the world—in all of these ways, evangelicals demonstrate the closed-mindedness of their faith, and thus also its political illiberalism.

In recent years, some have detected signs of change—hints of increasing liberality of spirit—in the evangelical community. Sociologist Alan Wolfe has spoken of an "opening of the evangelical mind" at some traditionalist Protestant colleges and universities.[47] Even Mark Noll, an especially severe critic of evangelicalism's anti-intellectualism, has begun to sound more optimistic, writing about evangelical efforts to recover and appropriate the humanistic aspects of historic Christianity that they have tended to neglect. In these efforts, some evangelicals have begun to express admiration for Roman Catholic examples of intellectuality, which is itself an encouraging sign, not only because over the centuries Catholics have thought so deeply about the difficulties involved in negotiating between reason and revelation, but also because the willingness to engage in serious dialogue with Catholics demonstrates increasing broad-mindedness among historically anti-Catholic evangelicals.[48]

Non-evangelicals should be cheered by these developments and do what they can to encourage them. But they should not kid themselves about the difficulties that confront evangelical reformers. Attempting to steer a community as large and diffuse as evangelical Protestantism in a new direction would always be a daunting task. But it is especially challenging in this case because anti-intellectualism is so deeply ingrained in evangelical culture—and because the egalitarian commitments that foster that anti-intellectualism are so deeply ingrained in America's civic self-understanding.

IV

The Perils
of Providential Thinking

T ake a moment to ponder the monumental consequences of
inches. The young Adolf Hitler was wounded in the leg during the battle of the Somme. Had the shell fragment struck
him several inches higher, in the chest or head, he might well have
died in 1916, sparing humanity the Second World War and the Holocaust. In this alternative reality, tens of millions of men and women
who died on the battlefield, in aerial bombardment, and in concentration camps likely would have survived the 1930s and 1940s. They and
their descendants would have created a world different from our own
in innumerable and incalculable ways, both good and bad.

Why did history take one path and not the other? To the believer
in divine providence, the answer is obvious: because God willed it (or
perhaps because He willed not to intervene in the ordinary course of
events). From that premise, providential speculation begins, proposing any number of theories designed to explain why God would want
history to turn out the way it did—why it served God's purposes for

Hitler to survive while the direct and indirect victims of his actions died by the millions.

The secular historian approaches the question very differently. He or she might be able to write a history that identifies various social, cultural, political, economic, and personal causes of Hitler's rise to power—causes that might even go a long way toward explaining why the events of the 1930s and 1940s unfolded in the way they did. But to the question of why Hitler escaped death in the First World War, the secular historian has no answer beyond the seemingly banal remark that he survived because the shell fragment happened to miss his vital organs—because on that day, at that moment, Hitler got lucky. And that is all.

The apparent banality of the remark is a result of its obviousness to many of us—products as we are of a largely secular intellectual culture, inculcated in our public schools and universities (not to mention in middlebrow History Channel documentaries), that constantly highlights the role of chance in history. But in fact there is nothing obvious or trite about such an assumption. On the contrary, it is quite rare in the history of (at least) the West.

Much more common is the view, expressed in passages of both the Hebrew and Christian Bibles, that God knows and cares about each and every one of us—perhaps even about each and every hair on each and every one of our heads. It is an awesome thought, at once comforting and terrifying, to imagine the creator of the universe taking an interest in everything we say and do, think and feel. Even more overwhelming is the thought of God intervening in our lives to reward our righteousness and punish our wickedness, both individually and collectively. Yet the scriptural sources are clear: God takes an interest in the affairs of human beings, and since many of those affairs are communal, He plays a decisive role in our collective endeavors, including politics. The most historically consequential example of divine intervention in the political fate of a nation is, of course, God's covenant with ancient Israel, but it is hardly the only one. Indeed, most theologians over the centuries have agreed that God's providence extends, in some way, to all nations. Some, like Augustine and John Calvin, have even gone as far as to suggest that absolutely everything that happens in temporal affairs is directly willed by God.

From the time of the first Puritan settlements in colonial New England, Americans have eagerly speculated about the nation's role in God's purposes.[1] Sometimes they have worried that the country would be punished for its moral transgressions. Far more often, they have been inspired by the prospect of receiving God's favor and protection. These expressions of faith in God's providential guidance of our individual and collective lives tend to attract little notice precisely because they are so ubiquitous. Yet there are exceptions, as when Pat Robertson and the late Jerry Falwell described the terrorist attacks of September 11, 2001, as acts of divine punishment for the sinful behavior of feminists and homosexuals, or when the Rev. John Hagee proposed more recently that God used Hitler and the Holocaust as a means to bring about the founding of the state of Israel. These examples of providential reflection provoked public outcry, demonstrating that it has become highly controversial in the twenty-first-century United States to portray God as either vengefully punishing sin or engaging in brutal utilitarian calculus—permitting and perhaps even willing the suffering and slaughter of millions—in order to bring about His desired ends.

However offensive these pronouncements were to some, the fact is that they were perfectly representative examples of American providential thinking. Such thinking invariably highlights an event in history (the Puritan landfall in Massachusetts, the American founding, the establishment of Israel, the West's victory in the Cold War, the September 11 attacks) and seeks to explain it in terms of God's inten-

tions, the presumption being that nothing in history happens without
a reason that can be traced to the agency of the divine. Indeed, in
their theological assumptions the controversial assertions of Robertson, Falwell, and Hagee are indistinguishable from widely admired
public statements of American presidents from George Washington
through George W. Bush and beyond. All of them assume a purposive
movement of history. All of them assume that God plays a crucially
important and perhaps exclusive role in directing this movement.
And all of them assume that the United States is of decisive importance to the unfolding of the divine plan.

Americans have long been comfortable making these assumptions.
What they have found it exceedingly difficult to imagine is the possibility of divine indifference to the United States and its experiment
in self-government. Whether speculating about God's relationship to
human history from the pulpit or the office of the president—and
whether undertaking that speculation using the Calvinist concepts
that have long dominated our national culture or the alternative theological ideas proposed by less mainstream traditions—Americans
have presumed the nation worthy, perhaps uniquely worthy, of divine
attention. And that is a problem.

1

Every nation thinks of itself as special in some way. Without this presumption, there would be no patriotism, which can rarely be reduced
to a blind and bigoted attachment to one's own for its own sake. I
love my country not simply because it is mine, but also and more
fundamentally because I believe that what is mine is uniquely good,
uniquely worthy of being loved. Some nations trace their singular
goodness to glorious battles waged and won in a mythical past. Others emphasize the beauty of the country's landscape or the cultural

achievements of its citizens. Still others look up to gods or godlike founders whose example serves permanently to edify and enlighten the nation.

Many political communities, including the United States, combine these and other forms of patriotic self-regard, but America is unique in uniting them with a peculiarly Protestant style of theological reflection—one that portrays the nation as singularly blessed by the one true God. From the time of the earliest colonies down to today, remarkably large numbers of Americans have believed not only that God would watch out for and protect the nation but also that God has special plans for the United States—plans that may even include electing America to serve as a new Israel, empowered by God to bring democracy, liberty, and Christian redemption to the world. To employ Lincoln's famous phrase, Americans have often thought of themselves as an "almost chosen people."[2] It is this persistent theological self-confidence (some would say overconfidence) that distinguishes American patriotism from expressions of communal feeling in any other modern nation.

As with so many other aspects of American culture, the country's dominant view of providence has its roots in the Calvinism of the Puritans who settled New England in the early seventeenth century. Theologically speaking, Calvinists throughout northern Europe strongly emphasized the absolute sovereignty of God, which implied that God ultimately controls all events in the natural world and human history. In the exacting language of the Presbyterian Church's Westminster Confession of Faith (1649), "God, the great Creator of all things, doth uphold, direct, dispose, and govern all creatures, actions, and things, from the greatest to the least, by His most wise and holy providence."[3] The various Protestant groups that affirmed these and other similarly austere theological doctrines longed to establish a purified Christian church independent of existing ecclesiastical institutions. In England, this desire placed these "Puritans" and other Christian separatists at odds with both the Roman Catholic and Anglican churches, resulting at several points during the late sixteenth and early seventeenth centuries in civil unrest and violent persecution.

Many of the radical Calvinists who resolved to leave England to establish colonies in the newly discovered continent of North America believed themselves to be reenacting the exodus of the Hebrews from bondage in ancient Egypt. Having freely joined in a covenant with God and resolved to build a purified church and holy city in the New World, the Puritans boarded their ships confident that the Lord would guide and protect them on their "errand into the wilderness."[4] When William Bradford stepped off the *Mayflower* in 1620, he quoted Jeremiah: "Come let us declare in Zion the word of God." Ten years later, John Winthrop wrote in the midst of his voyage to America, "The work we have in hand, it is by mutual consent through a special overruling providence . . . to seek out a place of cohabitation and consorting under a due form of government both civil and ecclesiastical."[5] Once they established the New England colonies, many of the leading Puritans became more convinced than ever that it was within their communities that the Lord would "create a new heaven, and a new earth, new churches, and a new commonwealth together."[6]

It didn't turn out that way, of course, as conflicts and dissent within the colonies led to numerous schisms, expulsions, and the eventual dilution of the strenuous Puritan ethic. Yet the idea that the original colonists had come, with God's aid and assistance, to establish a "new Israel" on American shores managed to persist. Late in the seventeenth century, Cotton Mather claimed that John Winthrop had been "picked out for the work" of founding New England "by the provident hand of the most high," while William Bradford was a "Moses" who happily served as "an instrument" of the Almighty in establishing "Israel in America."[7]

Having made the basic analogy between Puritan New England and ancient Israel, some extended the comparison even further, to speculate about the perhaps decisive place of the American colonies in sacred history. In Calvinist interpretations of the Hebrew Bible, Israel was usually portrayed as a nation chosen by God to preserve His law until His son arrived to purify and promulgate it throughout the world. Israel was thus a divine crucible and a providential conduit for the gospels. So, it seemed, was America—a nation chosen by God to proclaim the re-pristinized Christianity of the Protestant Reformation to all peoples. Hence Puritan writer Edward Johnson's assertion in 1654 that the New England settlers were "forerunners of Christ's army," poised to announce to the nations of the world "the near approach of the most wonderful works that ever the sons of man saw."[8]

Early in the eighteenth century, the vision of America as a new Israel specially chosen by God to perform a divine mission was primarily limited to the Puritan and post-Puritan elite of New England. But by the middle of the century, the more modest views of providence that until that time had dominated throughout the mid-Atlantic and southern colonies had been supplanted by the stringent Calvinism of Massachusetts and Connecticut. America was New Englandized.[9] According to historian John F. Berens, the motor behind this extraordinary transformation was the Great Awakening of the 1740s, which helped to spread theological concepts throughout the colonies. In the electrifying sermons of George Whitefield, Jonathan Edwards, Gilbert Tennent, Samuel Davies, and many other preachers, colonists from New York to South Carolina encountered for the first time the potent providential ideas that had previously transfixed the minds of the Puritan settlers of New England.

Not that these ideas were identical to the ones that originally inspired John Winthrop, Cotton Mather, and other seventeenth-century writers. On the contrary, American providential thinking evolved dramatically as it circulated throughout the colonies. As Berens notes, the French and Indian War (1754–63), which followed immediately on the heels of the Great Awakening, contributed decisively to the transformation. For the first time, Americans began to define themselves in contrast to a vision of tyranny—namely, the (political and religious) absolutism of Catholic France. Unlike France, they concluded, the American colonies were a bastion of political and religious freedom. This freedom had been won, moreover, with the help of God's providence, which would continue to protect the colonies in times of danger, provided the colonists proved themselves worthy of it by maintaining their divinely favored civil and religious institutions. In Berens's words, by 1763—a full thirteen years before the signing of the Declaration of Independence and the outbreak of war with Great Britain over the supposedly tyrannical usurpations of King George III—the "ever-increasing *intercolonial* conviction that America was the New Israel" had come to mean that the colonies "had been assigned a providential mission somehow connected to the advancement of civil and religious freedom."[10]

Through the Revolutionary War, the years surrounding the ratification of the federal Constitution, and the early national period, pastors and presidents repeatedly praised the "great design of providence" that had led to the creation of a country dedicated to protecting and preserving political and religious liberty.[11] What were once the rather extreme theological convictions dominating a handful of rustic outposts on the edge of a wholly undeveloped continent were now the unifying and motivating ideology of a rapidly expanding and industrializing nation. Whatever difficulties the new nation faced—from the traumas of the War of 1812 to the gradual escalation of regional hostilities that ultimately issued in the Civil War—Americans remained remarkably confident that God was committed to the survival and success of its experiment in free government and would continue to intervene providentially in its affairs to ensure that outcome.

This confidence received an additional boost from the Second Great Awakening, which swept through wide swaths of the new nation in the early decades of the nineteenth century. Many of those caught up in the intense revivalistic fervor of the time became convinced that they were living through the last days of human history prior to the advent of a thousand-year reign of Christian peace and prosperity on earth. Millennial hopes and fears left long-lasting marks on older sects (like the Baptists and Methodists) and inspired the founding of eccentric new ones (like the Mormons and Seventh-Day Adventists). But they also added an eschatological dimension to American thinking about providence. What if God had created the United States to serve as the model for millennial perfection that would prefigure the Second Coming of Christ? Such questions had titillated the minds of American Christians since the time of the Puritans, but they began to be posed with renewed vigor as millennial passions reached unprecedented heights in the 1810s and 1820s.[12]

The ideology of "manifest destiny" that emerged in the 1840s and inspired the policy of westward expansion through the remainder of the century was an outgrowth of this newly millennarian form of Calvinist providentialism.[13] The man who coined the term, journalist John L. O'Sullivan, insisted that it was "by the right of our manifest destiny to overspread and to possess the whole of the continent which providence has given us for the great experiment of liberty and federated self-government."[14] Decades later, after the closing of the frontier, writer Robert Ellis Thompson penned a study of *The Hand of God in American History*, which likewise proclaimed that from the time of the first settlements to the Spanish–American War God had "shaped the course of our national history for His own ends."[15] It was a sentiment amplified by statesman–historian Albert J. Beveridge in

a speech before the US Senate in which he voiced unambiguous support for American annexation of the Philippines. As far as Senator
Beveridge was concerned, God

> has given us the spirit of progress to overwhelm the forces of
> reaction throughout the earth. He has made us adept at govern-
> ment that we may administer government among savage and
> senile peoples. Were it not for such a force as this the world
> would relapse into barbarism and night. And of all our race He
> has marked the American people as His chosen nation to finally
> lead in the redemption of the world.[16]

Economic and scientific progress directed by God and actualized by
Americans, divinely ordained political accomplishments issuing in
divinely sanctioned global hegemony by the United States, and God's
election of America to redeem the world—these were the essential elements of American providence at the dawn of the twentieth century.

Over subsequent decades, as the political, economic, military, and
cultural power of the United States expanded beyond anyone's expectations, providential thinking continued to play an important role in
defining American national identity and in setting the terms of public
debate. Woodrow Wilson's foreign policy outlook, including his proposal for a League of Nations that would make possible an era of global
perpetual peace, grew out of his strong faith in America's providential
role in the world. The Second World War's propaganda campaign frequently appealed to identical convictions. And politicians from both
political parties regularly cast the Cold War as a quasi-eschatological
conflict between the forces of darkness and light, with God clearly
standing on America's side of the battle. Even Adlai Stevenson, the
Democratic Party's answer to the "anti-intellectualism" of Dwight D.
Eisenhower, spoke unapologetically in 1952 about the "awesome mis-

sion" that "God has set for us," which was nothing less than "the leadership of the free world."[17] In more recent years, the cadences of the Calvinist consensus could be heard in Ronald Reagan's rhetorical evocations of America as a "city on a hill" and George W. Bush's frequent assurances that history moves in a "visible direction, set by liberty and the author of liberty"—showing that nearly four centuries after the Puritan settlers first made landfall on the coast of Massachusetts, providential thinking maintains a remarkably strong hold on the American imagination.[18]

2

For most of American history, the Roman Catholic Church quietly dissented from the nation's Calvinist consensus. There were many reasons for its reticence. To begin with, Catholics often viewed this consensus, and not without reason, as a cover for anti-Catholic bigotry. For most Americans—or at least those whose descendants arrived before the middle of the nineteenth century—the United States was a Protestant nation whose non-Protestant citizens fit uneasily into its providential story. Throughout the nineteenth century, the nation's public schools actively inculcated a highly exclusionary version of this story, relegating non-Protestants in general, and Catholics in particular, to the periphery. As far as the public schools were concerned, the God of Reformation Christianity had abundantly blessed the United States not because of but despite the nation's willingness to permit these non-Protestants to practice and perpetuate their doctrinally offensive faith within American borders.[19]

Then there was the Catholic Church's enormous size and scope. Although American Protestants, like all Christians, ultimately traced their faith back to the death of Jesus Christ in Jerusalem nearly two thousand years in the past, the Reformation's break from the institution of the Roman church had the effect of cutting off Protestant churches from that broader history. This was especially true on this side of the Atlantic, where distance from Europe had the effect of making the nation's rapidly proliferating Protestant denominations distinctively American in numerous ways, not least in their enthusiastic endorsement of American providentialism.[20] However much individual Catholics may have sympathized with—and occasionally succumbed to—the urge to participate in providential thinking about the United States, the Catholic Church in America remained a provincial outpost of a global institution unwilling to sanction the young nation's desire to see itself as decisively important to the unfolding of sacred history.[21] That Protestants in the United States also tended to assert that God approved of America's attachment to liberal–democratic ideals only increased the skepticism of a church officially and at times adamantly opposed to political reform in Europe.[22]

All of this began to change by the mid-1950s. These were the years of Catholicism's belated assimilation into the American cultural and political mainstream. It was also the time when the United States consolidated its status as a global power, making American providential musings less worthy of immediate dismissal by devout Christians from other parts of the world.[23] And then there was John Courtney Murray, the American Jesuit whose thought contributed so much to shaping the debate around religious freedom at the Second Vatican Council. In a series of academic articles during the 1950s and in his now-classic book *We Hold These Truths* (1962), Murray made three interrelated claims with important implications for providential thinking among American Catholics. First, he argued that the Vatican's historical opposition to democracy, toleration, and liberalism arose in understandable reaction to the anticlerical character of these concepts in continental European politics since the French Revolution. Second, he claimed that these concepts had taken a very different form in the United States—one far more accommodating to religion in general and to Catholicism in particular. Third and most contentiously, Murray asserted (as we saw above) that in their benign American form, these concepts ultimately derived from medieval Christianity—in other words, from the Catholic Church. Murray sincerely believed that the United States had (in the words of historian Patrick Allitt) "preserved the political–philosophical heritage of medieval Christendom better than any European nation, even the ostensibly Catholic monarchies of France and Spain."[24] That the Catholic political tradition "should have so largely languished in the so-called Catholic nations of Europe at the same time that its enduring vigor was launching a new republic across the broad ocean" was, Murray admitted, one of the great "ironies of history." But it was true nonetheless. Despite a long history of thinking "of its own genius in Protestant terms," the United States "owed its origins and the stability of its political structure" to a different tradition—the Catholic tradition.[25]

In making his case, Murray pointed to three aspects of Catholic–Christian consensus in the United States. The first he described as the nearly universal belief of Americans in the "sovereignty of God over society as well as over individual men."[26] Whether or not Murray intended his readers to hear echoes of the Calvinist doctrine of God's sovereignty, the contrast between the two views is instructive. For Calvin and his American followers, the term referred to God's direct, uniform, and regular guidance of nature and human history, as well as to His occasional acts of miraculous intervention. Murray's position, derived from the medieval theologian Thomas Aquinas, was very different, emphasizing that in most cases God exercises his sovereignty over human affairs indirectly, through the mediation of law. Nearly all Americans, for example, affirm the supposedly self-evident truths enunciated in the Declaration of Independence—truths about human equality and inalienable rights. It is these truths that ground the American Constitution and other positive laws. Yet those truths are grounded in something more fundamental—in what the Declaration calls "nature and nature's God." American positive law, in Murray's view, is grounded in the natural moral law, which is itself ultimately grounded in the divine law of God. The American republic was therefore "conceived in the tradition of natural law" enunciated and developed by the leading theologians of the Catholic Church.[27]

The second mark of continuity between the United States and the Catholic tradition, according to Murray, is America's emphasis on the consent of the governed. Indeed, Murray even goes so far as to make the astonishing claim that the principle of consent was "inherent in the medieval idea of kingship." America's supposedly unprecedented attempt to break from traditional notions of political hierarchy and found a society on more egalitarian ideals was therefore much less radical than it was usually claimed to be. It was "medieval society," in fact, that first upheld the "principle" that "there is a sense of justice inherent in the people." It was this principle that inspired the "American consensus" about "the capacity of the people to govern themselves."[28] Once again Americans proved themselves unintentionally to be functional Catholics.

The third and final link between the medieval Catholic Church and modern America, in Murray's view, is the latter's revival of the "distinction between state and society, which had perished [in Europe] under the advance of absolutism." Interestingly, Murray interprets this fundamental tenet of political liberalism—the view that certain private areas of life should be off-limits to government power or oversight—in a distinctly illiberal way, insisting that "only a virtuous people can be free," and thus that the state has a compelling interest in inculcating moral rectitude in its citizens to ensure that they not merely do what they *want* to do but, more importantly, what they *ought* to do.[29] This, for Murray, is "the American ideal of ordered freedom"—an ideal derived, like the Bill of Rights itself, from the "tradition of natural law," which is itself a "product of Christian history." When viewed in the light of this tradition and history, American democracy looks less like a "political experiment" in self-government grounded in the sovereignty of the people than a "spiritual and moral enterprise" specially keyed to the eternal verities revealed by the Catholic Church.[30]

Murray Catholicized the American past and then insisted he had merely unearthed what was there all along. It was a bold and clever tactic, and one that has influenced several prominent Catholic thinkers of the theoconservative right over the past few decades, most prominent among them the late Richard John Neuhaus, Michael Novak, George Weigel, and Robert P. George.[31] These writers share Murray's conviction that the survival of American democracy depends on citizens of the United States coming to think of "the Fathers of the Church and the Fathers of the American Republic" as seamlessly compatible in their political teachings. In the view of Murray and his acolytes, it was a "greatly providential blessing" that made such a synthesis possible throughout much of American history.[32] Whether such blessings would continue into the future remained an open question for Murray, just as it remains one for his admirers today.[33]

3

America's Protestant mainstream has tended to view the United States as directly chosen by God for a special mission contributing in some decisive way to his divine plan for human history. Catholic providential thinking has been somewhat more restrained, pointing to the supposed natural-law foundations of American ideals and institutions—foundations through which God has indirectly revealed the form of government that most closely conforms with Catholic–

Christian moral teaching. But these hardly exhaust the alternatives. From the time of its founding in 1830 by Joseph Smith in upstate New York, Mormonism has proposed a uniquely radical doctrine of American providence. Taking the Calvinist emphasis on election several steps further than even its most fervent adherent has ever dared to do, the Mormons place the United States at the focal point of sacred history, treating it as "God's base of operations" in the world—a "great and glorious nation with a divine mission and a prophetic history and future."[34]

According to the founder of Mormonism, God had very good reasons for choosing the United States as the place where authentic Christianity would be restored. Smith produced a 500-page document, *The Book of Mormon*, containing the record of an ancient civilization, descended from the biblical Israelites, that supposedly lived, flourished, and collapsed in the Americas one thousand years before the arrival of Christopher Columbus. Jesus Christ visited these people after his resurrection in Jerusalem, spreading his gospel in the New World and planting the seeds of its rebirth many centuries later by Smith himself.

The Book of Mormon is filled with passages singling out the Americas as a " 'land of promise,' chosen and blessed above all others."[35] Readers are assured that the American Zion was destined by divine providence to "be a land of liberty," one that God promised in the distant past to "fortify . . . against all other nations."[36] Centuries before the arrival of the first Puritan settlers, God supposedly ordained that one day the "Gentiles" would "be set up as a free people by the power of the Father" on American shores, and that "these things might come forth from them unto a remnant of your seed, that the covenant of the Father may be fulfilled which He hath covenanted with His people, O house of Israel."[37] As long as the future inhabitants of this "choice land" humbly served "the God of the land, who is Jesus Christ," they would be guaranteed to remain "free from bondage, and from captivity, and from all other nations under heaven."[38] That, according to Mormon scripture, was God's sacred promise to the United States.

In later revelations, Smith went even further in highlighting the importance of the United States to God's plans for the world. The Garden of Eden, he claimed, was located in Jackson County, Missouri. The American constitutional framers were "raised up" by God in order to establish a free government that would allow the restoration to occur and the LDS church to spread the restored gospel throughout the nation and the world.[39] (Accordingly, all 30,000 undergraduates at LDS-owned Brigham Young University are required to take "American Heritage," a course that teaches "the American system of government and institutions in the context of the Restored Gospel.")

The centrality of the United States to Mormon theology extends beyond the past and present to encompass the End Times as well. Like many of the religious groups to emerge from the Second Great Awakening of the early nineteenth century, the early Mormons were millennarians who believed themselves to be living through the final years of ordinary human history; hence the words "latter-day" in the church's official title. Where the LDS differed from other communities gripped by eschatology, however, was once again in the vital role they envisioned the United States playing in the End Times. Whereas the Puritans and many other devout American Protestants followed Calvin in affirming "postmillennialism"—the belief that Christ's Second Coming would follow a thousand-year epoch of Christian peace and prosperity—the Mormons were emphatically "premillennial," meaning that they believed that Christ would return prior to the advent of the millennial Golden Age. The difference is crucial. From the time of the Puritan landing in Massachusetts, postmillennialism has been consistent with the widespread belief that American achievements have been providentially ordained by God as a preparation for the return of Christ, which will take place at some undetermined time in the (perhaps distant) future. The premillennialism of the Mormons, by contrast, has tended to hold that upon Christ's imminent return he will reign "personally upon the earth" for one thousand years—most likely from within "Zion," which Smith confidently equated with "the whole of America."[40]

These theological convictions, combined with the experience of persistent, severe persecution at the hands of their fellow citizens, led Smith and his followers to view American politics as a stage on which the ultimate divine drama was likely to play itself out, with Smith himself in the leading role.[41] In the months leading up to his June 1844 murder at the hands of a mob in Carthage, Illinois, Smith decided that God wanted him to establish a political kingdom (which he described as a "theodemocracy") to anticipate and prepare the way for the millennium.[42] To this end, Smith formed an ecclesiastical–political body called the Council of Fifty that quickly ordained him "a king, to reign over the house of Israel forever."[43] According to historian and Smith biographer Richard Bushman, the council's unelected members considered the institution to be "the incipient organization for millennial rule, a shadow government awaiting the demise of worldly political authority and the beginning of Christ's earthly reign." As such it was "an initial step toward establishing government for the Kingdom of God."[44]

The formation of the council was only part of Smith's eschatological plans, which also involved him petitioning Congress to raise a 100,000-man army and running for president of the United States. Smith's quixotic presidential campaign, cut short by an assassin's bullet just weeks after it was announced, had little influence on the November 1844 election. But while it lasted, it appeared to many Mormons to be yet another step on the road to Christ's "redemption of Zion"—and additional confirmation that Smith was already (in the words of early Mormon leader Lyman Wight) the "president pro tem of the world."[45]

Although the LDS church has moderated considerably in the years since Smith's assassination, giving up several of its most unusual practices and moving a considerable distance into the American religious and political mainstream, its unique beliefs about American providence live on at the level of Mormon culture and folklore. No LDS belief about God's providence is more controversial and widespread than the notion, rooted in a prophecy delivered by Joseph Smith in May 1843, that at some mysterious and cataclysmic moment in the future the US Constitution will "hang by a thread" only to be saved by a Mormon who will then miraculously transform the nation into "the Zion of God."[46] Some LDS church officials deny the veracity of this prophecy, but it has been affirmed as genuine by a long line of prominent Mormons and church leaders, including Brigham Young, Joseph F. Smith, Charles Penrose, J. Reuben Clark, Joseph Fielding Smith, and Harold B. Lee.[47] More recently, Republican senator Orrin Hatch of Utah raised eyebrows in the Mormon community when he declared, on an LDS-owned radio station in the midst of his failed 2000 campaign for president, "I've never seen it worse than this, where the Constitution literally is hanging by a thread."[48] There can be little doubt that Hatch was attempting to rally the Mormon faithful to his side by raising the prospect that his election to the White House would fulfill Smith's political prophecy and signal the advent of the Mormon millennium in America.[49]

4

Providential thinking has thus been widespread in American history, transcending the boundaries that separate otherwise divergent faith communities, and it continues to play an important role in our time, regularly echoing through the public utterances of prominent preachers and politicians. Principled criticism of American providentialism, by contrast, has been rare. In attempting to formulate a critique of our own, one option is to follow the lead of political theorist Isaiah Berlin in casting doubt on all accounts of purposiveness in history. Berlin readily conceded how rarely human beings have affirmed a contingent view of history: "The notion that history obeys laws, whether natural or supernatural, that every event in human life is an element in a necessary pattern, has deep metaphysical origins." Its roots "reach back to the beginning of human thought," and its branches wend their way through the premodern philosophical tradition, the theological speculations of the monotheistic religions, and even the dialectical materialism of doctrinaire Marxism.

As Berlin goes on to explain, those who adhere to this teleological outlook presume that in order to make history intelligible, they must "reveal the basic pattern" that lies behind the "succession of events"— "not one of several possible patterns, but the one unique plan, which . . . fulfills only one particular purpose." Once this purpose has been identified, the otherwise random succession of events can be assimilated into "the single 'cosmic' schema which is the goal of the universe, the goal in virtue of which alone it is a universe at all, and not a chaos of unrelated bits and pieces." According to Berlin, a teleological interpretation of history gains its power to assimilate these seemingly unrelated historical fragments into a purposive cosmic whole by emphasizing *inevitability*: "The more inevitable an event or an action or a character can be exhibited as being, . . . the nearer we are to the one embracing, ultimate truth."[50]

Berlin spends most of his time in his seminal essay on "Historical Inevitability" attacking such theories for relieving human beings of moral responsibility. As he writes, "to think that there exists *the* pattern, *the* basic rhythm of history . . . is to commit oneself to the view that . . . individual responsibility is, 'in the end,' an illusion." It is to accept the view that human beings are mere "puppets" manipulated by mysterious forces beyond our control. And though these puppets "may be conscious and identify themselves happily with the inevitable process in which they play their parts," this process "remains inevitable, and they remain marionettes" in the hands of occult powers that guide and direct their actions.[51] All such historical theories—including providential theories of history—end up serving as "alibis, pleaded by those who cannot or do not wish to face the fact of human responsibility."[52]

It is a powerful criticism, albeit one that is far more effective against Marxist historical determinism, which Communist governments readily used to justify their totalitarian social policies, than it is against the kinds of providentialism proposed by the greatest theologians in the Christian tradition, who took the matter of human moral responsibility very seriously. (As a thoroughly secular thinker who addressed himself to a thoroughly secular audience, Berlin felt no obligation to engage religious arguments.) More effective is Berlin's attempt to clarify what kind of thinking providentialism really is. Treating American belief in "manifest destiny" as a prime example, Berlin describes providential thinking as a "metaphysical attitude which takes for granted that to explain a thing . . . is to discover its purpose." This means that teleology "is not a theory, or a hypothesis, but a category or a framework in terms of which everything is, or should be, conceived or described." Teleology is thus a "form of faith," one capable "of neither confirmation nor refutation by any kind of experience"—or at least by any experience short of an undemonstrable, nonreproducible divine revelation.[53] Providential thinking is therefore "profoundly anti-empirical"—merely one form of the unsubstantiated myths that have dominated human cultures from the time of the earliest surviving historical records. For those who choose to live safely ensconced behind the walls created by such myths rather than breaking out to embrace the liberating complexity of the empirical world, Berlin has nothing but contempt: "Some human beings have always preferred the peace of imprisonment, a contented security, a sense of having at least found one's proper place in the cosmos, to the painful conflicts and perplexities of the disordered freedom of the world beyond the walls."[54]

One need not approve of Berlin's condescension to see that he has a point. Why have so many Americans upheld one or another doctrine of providence? Either because its truth has been revealed to them by God directly or (more likely) because they have decided to accept its truth on faith, trusting in the validity of someone else's revelation. Berlin's secularist critique of this reliance on revealed truth boils down to an affirmation of skepticism. Don't we all, even the most pious among us, recognize that some putative revelations ultimately prove to be false? And isn't it obvious that some accounts of other people's experiences turn out to be exaggerated and embellished, sometimes deliberately, but oftentimes unintentionally, as a result of pride, faulty memory, or mistaken interpretations of the supposed revelation? The secularist believes that an honest and intelligent person will answer these questions in the affirmative—and that once this has happened, the case for the empirical (non-providential) study of history's contingencies has been made, as the only available means of determining the truth of the matter.

5

There is a more decisive objection to providential readings of history—more decisive because raised by authors writing from deep within the Christian tradition itself. Indeed, the first theologian to take a stand against those who sought to construct elaborate providential histories was none other than Augustine, the greatest of the Christian church fathers and an important inspiration behind the Protestant Reformation, including its emphasis on the absolute sovereignty of God. Augustine wrote his classic text *The City of God* partially as a response to the histories written by such Christian authors as Origen and Eusebius, who highlighted the role of the Roman Empire in providentially spreading Christianity throughout the known world. Eusebius was especially taken with the conversion of the emperor Constantine to Christianity, which he treated as definitive proof that God had chosen Rome to serve as a providential conduit for realizing His purposes in the world. It was a powerful and persuasive interpretation—at least while Rome maintained its preeminence. When the empire was invaded and the city sacked by the Visigoths in the year 410, the Eusebian equation of the fate of Rome with the fate of the church seemed to imply that Christianity, too, was under assault. Had God abandoned the faithful, withdrawing His guidance and protection?

Writing in the wake of the barbarian invasion of the empire and confronting this terrifying possibility, Augustine highlighted the ubiquity but also the mysteriousness of God's ways within the world. On the one hand, Christians must believe that God guides worldly events. Indeed, it is "incredible" to suppose that "the kingdoms of men" lie "outside the range of the laws of His providence."[55] On the other hand, it is impossible to know, or even to guess, God's reasons, which "are inscrutable," or His intentions, which infinitely surpass human understanding.[56] Hard as it might be for Christian citizens of Rome to accept, it was not their place to engage in Eusebian speculations. Rather, they should repeatedly pose the rhetorical question, "Who knows what is God's will in this matter?"[57] To suppose that such knowledge lies within our reach is to fall prey to sin—the sin of equating one's own passing moment in the flow of time for a privileged vantage point, for the eternal vantage point of God. Not only does this sin gravely distort one's judgment and unjustly exaggerate the importance of one's time and place in the order of creation, but it also ties the church too closely to the fallen and sinful world of politics, tempting Christians to find their salvation in the city of man—with its partisan pursuits and lust for power—instead of in the transcendent city of God that is our proper end.

It is a difficult balance to strike and maintain—believing in providence yet forbidden to draw practical conclusions from its mysterious path through history. With so much at stake—morally, spiritually, existentially—it's no wonder that so many Christians over the centuries have given into the temptation to read the tea leaves, setting themselves the impossible task of dusting for God's undetectable fingerprints in the temporal world. Americans have found it especially hard to restrain themselves from such providential endeavors. We are, it seems, a consummately un-Augustinian people, all too inclined toward what Alexis de Tocqueville appropriately described as the "perpetual utterance of self-applause."[58] What better way to give ourselves an ego boost than to imagine that God Himself is eager to lead a standing ovation in our honor?

How fortunate, then, that one of the twentieth century's leading Augustinian theologians happened to be an American who devoted much of his mature writing to penning a loving but severe Christian critique of his country's providential pretensions.[59] Reinhold Niebuhr's critical confrontation with American providentialism can be found in many passages of his work, but it was most fully developed in *The Irony of American History* (1952). "Every nation has its own form of spiritual pride," Niebuhr notes, and the American version takes the form of the myth that "our nation turned its back upon the vices of Europe and made a new beginning"—a beginning marked by moral purity and the special favor of God.[60] This uniquely American self-understanding has tended to inspire national overconfidence with

regard to our virtue.[61] Much of Niebuhr's book is devoted to examin-
ing the many ways this overconfidence manifests itself in American
thinking and actions.

Niebuhr maintains that American overconfidence makes us a
nation impatient with various limitations that are coeval with the
human condition. We are, first of all, impatient with limits on our
knowledge and power. Convinced that God is on our side, we lack
the humility to accept that "the whole drama of human history is
. . . too large for human comprehension or management."[62] We are
likewise impatient with limitations on the degree of moral purity—
especially our own—that is possible in political life. Niebuhr rightly
remarks that Americans nearly always mean well when they act in
the world. Our moral perils are thus "not those of conscious malice
or the explicit lust for power." Yet the rules of the world are such that
good intentions, even our own, often lead to unintended bad consequences. This is a lesson we seem incapable of learning, or remem-
bering, so eager are we to deny that the actions of even "the best men
and nations" are "curious compounds of good and evil."[63] And this
leads to a third, distinctly American form of impatience—one that
expresses itself in an attitude of impotent defiance toward "the slow
and sometimes contradictory processes of history." We desperately
want to believe that we are contributing to the realization of God's
plans for humanity, but we find it exceedingly difficult to accept that
the path humanity will take on the way to its appointed end is as
obscure to us as the precise shape of the end itself.[64]

Having imagined ourselves standing by God's side as His trusted
lieutenant, we half believe He has granted us wisdom and power
comparable to His. But this is folly, a prideful delusion as old as Genesis 3. In Niebuhr's view, America needs regularly self-administered
doses of humility. It needs to recognize that like the shapes discovered in the amorphous ink blots of a Rorschach test, patterns detected

in history are unavoidably subjective, reflecting the necessarily narrow standpoint of the person or nation proposing the interpretation. Seeing and judging the whole with accuracy transcends our meager powers, both because of our limited perspective and because of the passions, including self-love, that nearly always lead us to judge poorly when our own case is involved. All of which is why, according to Niebuhr, we must "moderate our conceptions of the ability of men and of nations to discern the future."[65]

The point is not that believers should abandon their faith that God plays a providential role in the world. It is that they should be circumspect about the practical conclusions they can draw from this faith. This is especially true for theologians and preachers, those who should know better than to encourage our pride and impatience—our longing to claim "God too simply as the sanctifier of whatever we most fervently desire." These Christian leaders need constantly to remind themselves that "the true God can be known only where there is some awareness of a contradiction between divine and human purposes, even on the highest level of human aspirations."[66] Only then can they fulfill their special responsibility to remind their fellow citizens that all theological meaning in history is and will remain provisional for the duration of our mortal lives, with its final meaning obscured by our limited vision.[67]

Politicians and other public figures—individuals whose decisions determine the course of history so much more than the rest of us—face special challenges. If they are believers themselves, they need to take the lessons of humility closely to heart and resist the temptation to view themselves as God's agents in history. To do otherwise—to view their policies as having been personally authored or approved by the divine—is foolishness that will tend to distort their judgment, inspiring the distinctly American overconfidence that Niebuhr warned against so powerfully. Then there is a different temptation—

one that needs to be resisted by believing and skeptical politicians alike. This is the urge to use providential rhetoric and the hopes and expectations it raises to mold and manipulate public opinion for the sake of political gain.

Many American politicians, from George Washington to George W. Bush, have succumbed to these temptations. Yet the case of Barack Obama may be different. Obama has frequently expressed his admiration for Niebuhr, and in his public rhetoric he clearly strives to follow in the footsteps of Abraham Lincoln—the public figure Niebuhr singles out for having left behind a public meditation on American providence that lives on to teach us by example. In his second inaugural address, delivered as the Civil War was at long last drawing to a close, Lincoln somehow managed to step back from his position as commander in chief of the Union army to achieve a broader perspective on the conflict as a whole. Rather than praising the North for its victory or denigrating the cause of the defeated South, Lincoln spoke in tones of irony—of each side's invocation of the blessings of the divine against the other. If providence was at work in the slaughter of the Civil War, it could be seen not, or not simply, in the triumph of the Union, but in the incalculable suffering of soldiers and citizens on both sides—as divine retribution for the national sin of slavery. But Lincoln did not permit even this humbling thought to serve as a consolation. For not even this possible theological meaning of the slaughter, or its ultimate outcome, could be known with any certainty. All the nation could do was hope and pray for an end to the conflict, and humbly accept whatever providence might bring.

Lincoln thus managed to invoke the idea of providence while avoiding the vices it so often encourages—which is why Niebuhr described the speech as an "almost perfect model of the difficult but not impossible task of remaining loyal and responsible toward the moral treasures of a free civilization . . . while yet having some religious vantage point over the struggle."[68] It was a considerable achievement, and one that our current president apparently wishes to emulate, especially in his speeches to foreign audiences.[69] It remains to be seen how the American people will respond, conditioned by history and habit to expect their leaders to flatter them and the nation, and encouraged by populist rabble-rousers on talk radio, cable news, and the Internet to view any expression of providential modesty as evidence of weakness and even deep-seated anti-Americanism. If Obama pays a political price for seeking to rein in America's theologically inflated vision of itself, it will be a terrible shame—and an unfortunate sign that the United States continues to persist in a state of collective self-delusion, incapable of resigning itself to the humbling reality of human, and national, limits.

V

The Impossibility
of Sexual Consensus

What do religious traditionalists think about when they think about sex? To judge from the flurry of emails and blast faxes launched daily by the interdenominational coalition of religious groups that claims to speak for traditionalists, they think mostly about America—about what it was, is, and might be again.[1] The narrative goes something like this. Until the 1960s, the United States was an overwhelmingly traditionalist Christian nation in practice, belief, and aspiration—and these traditionalist Christian practices, beliefs, and aspirations were in many cases backed up by law. Abortion was strictly regulated, and often banned outright, for example, as was "sodomy"—a term that was used to describe, regulate, and prohibit all forms of non-procreative sex, from masturbation to oral and anal sex, whether practiced by members of the same or different genders, both inside and outside of marriage.

Beginning nearly five decades ago, the story continues, the default sexual traditionalism of the United States began to collapse—not because (as some have argued) large numbers of Americans were persuaded by moral arguments in favor of sexual liberation, and not because (as others have claimed) broader socioeconomic trends encouraged the growth of democratic individualism. According to most social conservatives, the sexual liberalization of the past several decades has instead been brought about through the organized effort of decadent liberal elites in the nation's education and media establishments to impose a hedonistic ethic on the country through antidemocratic means (especially through the courts, which have repeatedly overturned laws that previously regulated sexual behavior). The proper response to the spread of sexual decadence is thus to allow the country's religious traditionalism to reassert itself democratically—primarily by citizens voting for conservative Christian politicians who seek to turn back the changes of recent decades through public policy, court appointments, constitutional amendments, and referenda that frustrate the tyrannical ambitions of the hedonists.

The traditionalist outlook on sex gets a lot of things wrong.[2] Yet its champions are right about one crucially important matter: for much of its history, the United States did indeed conform in its practices, beliefs, and aspirations to the sexually traditionalist view of the world. Where social conservatives err is in asserting, often in conspiratorial tones, that this sexual traditionalism was a reflection of the nation's Christian essence—an essence that has been suppressed by the forces of secular hedonism but that will reassert itself at some point in the not too distant future. It is far more accurate to say, instead, that America's pre-sixties sexual traditionalism was the political and legal expression of a historically contingent cultural consensus—a consensus that over the past several decades has (for various complicated reasons) broken down, leaving rancor and dissent in its wake. Whereas the overwhelming majority of Americans once considered it appropriate for laws and mores to regulate private sexual conduct, somewhat less than half of the country supports such regulations today.

When a consensus is lacking in other areas of public policy—from environmental regulation to foreign affairs, from tax policy to health care reform—politicians often seek to reach a compromise, to settle on a position that responds to concerns voiced by those on both sides (or even on multiple sides) of a given issue. The polarizing sexual issues that form the explosive core of the culture war cry out for such civic conciliation, yet they frequently prove to be especially resistant to compromise. Pondered in the abstract, the cultural clash over same-sex marriage, for instance, seems like a conflict for which federalism would be the perfect solution: allow the handful of states (or even cities or regions) with the highest density of homosexuals to experiment with gay marriage while leaving traditional marriage untouched in the rest of the country.

In practice, however, such a political compromise is unworkable. The "full faith and credit" clause of the US Constitution quite sensibly insists that each state must recognize the "public acts, records, and judicial rulings" of other states, and that might very well include (and up to this point in history, it usually has included) marriages performed under differing state laws. Mississippi, for example, permits girls to marry beginning at age fifteen, which is earlier than many other states. Yet a fifteen-year-old girl who has been married in Mississippi remains married when she travels to or establishes residence in any other state, even one in which she is too young to have gotten married in the first place. It is likely that the same universalizing logic will eventually apply to same-sex marriages performed in Massachusetts, Vermont, New Hampshire, Maine, Iowa, Connecticut, or any other state that has legalized such marriages: judges will eventually conclude that the US Constitution demands their portability to other states, even those with laws explicitly banning same-sex marriage. Just as, legally speaking, the United States in the nineteenth century was destined to become "all one thing, or all the other" with regard to slavery, so it may very well be today with regard to gay marriage and the other polarizing sexual issues tied up with the culture war.[3]

At the moment, the possibility of achieving something close to total victory through a combination of evolving majority opinion and sympathetic court rulings is inspiring some same-sex marriage proponents and their allies in the culture war to gloat. A more appropriate response would be for less fervently religious Americans to adopt an attitude of magnanimity and respect toward sexual traditionalists—and not only because a ruthlessly defeated minority can still create an awful lot of political trouble, as we know all too well from the role that the strident *Roe v. Wade* abortion decision played in conjuring the religious right into existence during the 1970s and to an astonishing extent keeps it alive to this day. The more fundamental reason why civic-minded combatants on the liberal side of the cultural divide should respectfully engage their opponents is that such engagement is the approach most likely to persuade conservatives that the traditionalist consensus that once prevailed in the United States is thoroughly unrecoverable—and thus that the liberal position on the political deregulation of sex is our nation's only hope for conciliation.

1

Up until the past few decades, Americans, and indeed most men and women in the Western world, considered homosexual desires to be gravely evil and acting on them even worse. This judgment was accepted by nearly everyone, including most homosexuals themselves, many of whom lived lives shot through with shame, denial, and self-loathing. This is to say that on matters of sexuality Americans assumed a *morality of ends*: they assumed that certain ways of living and acting are right or wrong in themselves, intrinsically, with their

rightness or wrongness determined by the extent to which they conform to an ideal vision of humanity. One version of a morality of ends
is taught today by the Roman Catholic Church in an idiom derived
from the natural-law writings of Thomas Aquinas. Human sexuality,
the church claims, is ordered by God toward the end of procreation,
and sexual desires and activities that aim primarily toward other ends
(such as pleasure or intimacy) are essentially disordered and offensive to God—in a word, evil. Traditionalists from other churches,
now and in the past, may describe their beliefs in less philosophically
rigorous ways, but when they denounce homosexuality or any other
form of extramarital and/or non-procreative sex, they inevitably do so
in terms of some stated or implied morality of ends.

A traditionalist morality of ends with regard to sex was once
assumed by nearly all Americans. But that is no longer the case.
Does that leave us, as some on the religious right have argued, fighting an ideological civil war, with factions combating one another
over incompatible ends with no possible hope for finding common
ground?[4] While it might sometimes feel that way, the liberal political tradition has actually bequeathed to us another way of conceiv-
ing morality—one explicitly designed to enable people who disagree
about fundamental ends to live together in relative peace, harmony,
and mutual respect.[5]

The first liberal political theorists—men like Thomas Hobbes, John
Locke, and Montesquieu—wrote during or shortly following a time of
real civil wars, many of which pitted Protestants against Catholics as
well as various Protestant factions against each other in a series of
bloody conflicts throughout Europe. It was in response to this car-
nage that these writers proposed a new form of morality—a *morality
of rights*—that could be superimposed onto the divergent moralities
of ends that were driving Europeans to kill one another. The morality
of rights treats disagreement about ultimate ends as the normal con-

dition of social life and then seeks to find common ground shared by every faction within society, regardless of the ends they affirm or pursue. That common ground turns out to be a belief in individual dignity, and on its basis liberalism makes certain minimal but inviolable moral claims, among them the claim that individuals have rights to life and liberty. Most liberals have also added, whether explicitly or implicitly, certain rights that flow from the right to liberty, like rights to private property and the pursuit of whatever ends (including happiness, however defined) the individual affirms, provided that the pursuit of these ends does not infringe the equal rights of anyone else to do the same. In the liberal tradition, the morality of rights determines the relative size and scope of government. If the liberal state is too strong, it threatens to violate the individual rights of citizens; when it is too limited, it fails to defend the individual rights of citizens against violations by other individuals and groups within civil society.

A society based on the morality of rights looks very much like modern America, with the state protecting individual rights to life, liberty, and the pursuit of ultimate ends (happiness) but leaving it up to each individual to choose his or her ends in the expansive private lives opened up by limited government. Americans can be devout Protestants or atheists, orthodox Catholics or Unitarians, secular Jews or committed Mormons. They can choose to live in a racially homogeneous gated community or to protest with Martin Luther King, Jr. They can march for civil rights—or oppose those who march for civil rights—because they believe it is God's will that they do so, or they can make their decision based on purely secular considerations. They can live lives devoted to making money, or they can join the Peace Corps. They can believe that the United States is providentially blessed by Jesus Christ, or that it is an abomination in the eyes of God—or that it has unique humanitarian responsibilities in the world because of its power and ideals, or that it has no special responsibilities at all beyond policing its own borders. And so on, through nearly every alternative open to the roughly 300 million citizens of our metaphysically centerless society.

That's liberalism in action: politics without metaphysics. Not politics against metaphysics, as some illiberal atheists would apparently prefer, but politics conducted, as much as possible, in an idiom of metaphysical neutrality, taking no position for or against God—or for or against any particular views about God and what He might or might not want from human beings. Individuals are free to believe just about anything about their ultimate ends, provided that they give up the ambition to political rule in the name of those beliefs—that is, the ambition to use political power to bring the highly differentiated whole of social life into conformity with the ends affirmed by one part of that whole.

There is a problem with this vision of politics conducted according to the morality of rights, one that religious traditionalists frequently highlight in their efforts to use state power to bring the country into conformity with their views on sexuality. If liberal government adopts a stance of neutrality with regard to ultimate ends, the objection runs, how is it that the liberal United States so clearly sided with sexual traditionalism for so much of its history, permitting laws against sodomy throughout the country as well as countless laws regulating various aspects of sexual conduct, from the use of contraception to intercourse outside of heterosexual marriage? It's a crucially important question with far-reaching implications. In posing it, religious traditionalists wish to discredit political liberalism by proving that the ideal of metaphysical neutrality is a sham concealing liberalism's own metaphysical commitment to hedonistic self-expression, which it actively seeks to impose, using government power, on citizens with differing metaphysical views. That, according to the most intellectually formidable members of the religious right, is the primary reason

why the country has fallen away from its former traditionalism—
because nihilistic liberals have deposed the old order of traditional-
istic metaphysical commitments and replaced it with a new order
founded on contrary metaphysical commitments, all in the name of
metaphysical neutrality.[6]

The truth of the matter is much less conspiratorial than traditionalist critics would have us believe, and in fact provides compelling evidence of liberalism's remarkable flexibility and openness as a political
and moral system. Liberalism makes use of numerous political institutions to limit its own power and ensure the protection of individual
rights, one of which is the institution of democratic elections, which
reflect and respond to public opinion. Of course there will be (and
have been) times when public opinion (along with the laws legislatures write in response to public opinion) directly conflicts with the
individual rights the liberal state is empowered to protect. In such
cases, laws will often be overturned upon review by the independent
judiciary (another liberal institution). But what will happen when the
social and cultural consensus on a given matter is so strong that no
one (or very few), either in the nation at large or in the judicial branch
of government, objects to a law, even though it is grounded exclusively in a morality of ultimate ends? In such a situation, the law will
stand, despite its illiberalism.

This was obviously the situation in the United States until quite
recently with regard to laws enforcing sexual traditionalism. The tacit
consensus in favor of such laws was so universal that next to no one
challenged them in either the political or judicial branches of government. As long as this consensus held, illiberal traditionalist laws were
safe. But as soon as that consensus began to break down—as soon
as significant numbers of citizens began to make the case for sexual
freedom—the liberal state was ready to step into the gap separating
the parties, just as the first liberal theorists said it should do hundreds

of years ago in early modern Europe, offering to resolve a dispute by depoliticizing it. Traditionalists would henceforth be perfectly free to continue adhering to their beliefs, but those beliefs could no longer have the force of law because they now merely expressed the will of a *part* of society rather than the *whole* of society. Thus began the liberal state's inexorable retreat from enforcing a morality of ultimate ends in sexual matters—a retreat still very much under way.[7]

Today's sexual traditionalists are thus wrong to view themselves as victims of a liberal state hell-bent on spreading hedonism throughout the land. On the contrary, the very same liberal state was perfectly willing to enforce traditionalism's morality of ultimate ends so long as there was an overwhelming consensus among the American people in favor of that morality. It is the breakdown of that consensus in American *society*, and not the imperialistic ambitions of the liberal state, that has led to the depoliticization (and thus privatization) of sexual morality in the United States. The liberal state is not predisposed to defend and enforce sexual liberation; it is predisposed to stymie the efforts of a part of society to use state power to impose its vision on the whole of society.

2

Many sexual traditionalists view the prospect of same-sex marriage as the ultimate example of the liberal state explicitly turning against traditionalism, actively seeking its overthrow, and working to substitute a very different understanding of sexual relations. Where Americans once treated marriage as a solemn and sacred "one-flesh" union joining a man and woman together for life primarily for the sake of procreation, advocates for same-sex marriage would transform the institution into a contract open to any consenting individuals for any reason at all.[8] In this way, the traditionalist morality of ends that prevailed throughout the country (and throughout the Western world) for centuries would be replaced with an alternative morality of ends— one that denies the privileged status of traditional heterosexual marriage and opens the door to "marriages" among the members of polygamous or polyandrous groups, and perhaps even among the members of different species.[9]

As usual, the reality is much more complicated than traditionalists would have us believe. To begin with, marriage law in the United States has never described the institution in the explicitly religious terms favored by traditionalists. The state issues a marriage license, which establishes a contract between the parties. That is all. Where traditionalist considerations have historically played a role is in setting the terms of the contract—making it extremely difficult to dissolve, for example, as it nearly always was until reforms in divorce law during the 1970s.[10] Why were those reforms undertaken over the objection of traditionalists? The traditionalists themselves would likely say it was because that's when the liberationists of the sexual revolution finally gained enough power in the nation's political and cultural institutions to enforce their hedonistic morality of ultimate ends on the nation. In fact, however, divorce law was liberalized during the 1970s because nontraditionalist Americans began to feel that the state was sanctioning one (traditionalist) view of marriage while disregarding other (less traditionalist) religious practices and beliefs, not to mention widespread secular practices and beliefs. A part of society was attempting to impose its morality of ultimate ends on the whole of a society no longer unified in its views on sexuality and gender roles.

The other way that traditionalist views have typically asserted themselves in marriage law is in the religious norms, practices, and beliefs that traditionalists have brought to and superimposed on the civil marriage contract. The state empowers priests, ministers, rabbis, and imams, along with civil justices of the peace, to perform civil marriages. This mixing of sacred and secular allows traditionalists to treat a marriage as a profoundly spiritual event unfolding before the eyes of God, while also permitting nontraditionalists to take part in less formal procedures. But in both cases—the sacramental marriage officiated by an archbishop and the modest ceremony performed at city hall—the legal outcome is and always has been the same: a civil marriage contract.

And this will of course continue to be true if and when same-sex marriage comes to be legally accepted in every state of the union. In such an eventuality, traditionalists would be perfectly free to reject the legitimacy of same-sex marriage, to view it as an abomination in the eyes of God, and to perform wedding ceremonies that place procreation at the center of the institution and its moral and spiritual meaning. To be sure, the end result would be a marriage contract that is also open to same-sex couples. But the meaning of that contract would vary radically depending upon the moral and religious convictions of the parties involved—just as a man and woman married today in an Orthodox Jewish ceremony presumably understand their vows in dramatically different ways than a couple married in a nondenominational ceremony at a wedding chapel in Las Vegas. The liberal response to traditionalist concerns thus amounts to a variation on an old slogan: "Oppose same-sex marriage? Don't have one!"

Yet traditionalists claim this isn't good enough. In their view, the conferral of *private* meaning onto marriage is insufficient to keep this crucially important social institution alive and thriving. For that, traditional marriage must be *publicly* privileged. In the terms we have been using, traditionalists insist that the good of the United States demands that the nation as a whole set aside the morality of rights as it pertains to marriage and instead take a legal stand in favor of a particular morality of ultimate ends—the morality of ultimate ends espoused by sexual traditionalists.

There's just one problem with this position: it requires that the traditionalists mount public arguments in its defense, and thus far their efforts have been weak. Their arguments have been so weak, in fact, that they lead one to conclude not only that the traditionalist side is bound to lose its battle against same-sex marriage, but also that it deserves to lose.

The traditionalist argument usually begins with the assertion that the authoritative religious texts of Western civilization, along with thousands of years of tradition, confer a special exalted status on male–female unions while treating homosexual desires and activities as morally disgraceful. But the appeal to Scripture and tradition is obviously inadequate, even for most traditionalists themselves. The fact is that Scripture and tradition affirm the moral legitimacy of slavery, claim that the Jews are cursed for killing Jesus Christ, and assert that one must give away all of one's belongings and even learn to hate one's own family before following Christ. These are just a few of the matters on which contemporary Christians, traditionalist and nontraditionalist alike, feel quite comfortable breaking with, or explaining away, Scripture and tradition. And it's a good thing, too, because it shows that they're willing to think for themselves about important moral issues and to use their minds to separate out what might be enduringly true in Scripture and tradition from the unexamined prejudices that shape and distort everything touched by human hands, very much including received religious norms, practices, and beliefs. Traditionalists thus need to explain why they have decided that the scriptural and traditional teaching on marriage and homosexuality—but not the teachings on slavery, the Jews, and the most stringent requirements of becoming a disciple of Christ—deserves to be preserved and should be treated as normative for twenty-first century America as a whole.

Pushed to justify his appeal to Scripture and tradition, the traditionalist will often claim that heterosexuality is natural and homosexuality unnatural. This is a difficult argument to make, given all that
we now know about the pervasiveness of homosexual behavior in the
natural world.[11] So traditionalists usually insist that by "nature" they
mean that there is something fundamentally distinctive about *human*
nature that precludes homosexuality. And that something turns out
to be the transcendent end of procreation assigned to human beings
by their Creator. Viewed in this light, traditional marriage is special
because it orients human beings toward procreation and homosexuality is wrong because it is sexual activity cut off from the possibility
of procreation.

The argument is astonishingly weak, as prominent advocates for
gay rights have pointed out on numerous occasions.[12] For one thing,
the traditionalist argument would seem to undermine the naturalness
and moral legitimacy of marriages in which one or the other member
is sterile, including long-term marriages in which the woman has
entered menopause. Even more decisively, the procreative argument
implies that all non-procreative sexual activity—including masturbation, intercourse using contraception, and oral and anal sex, even
when engaged in by married couples—is unnatural and morally illegitimate. Without intending to, the traditionalist's effort to marginal-
ize homosexuals by appealing to the teleological end of procreation
has managed to exclude the vast majority of married heterosexuals
from the ranks of the natural and the morally acceptable.

Luckily for the traditionalists, conservative bioethicist Leon Kass
has proposed an alternative way to mount an argument about nature.
In his writings against cloning, Kass has suggested that we base our
moral arguments on what he calls "the wisdom of repugnance," by
which he means the visceral feeling of disgust elicited by thoughts
of cloning ourselves or others.[13] In Kass's view, this feeling indicates

that cloning transgresses a natural moral standard. A similar argument could be made about the unnaturalness of homosexuality, since many heterosexuals (especially men) find the idea of homosexual intercourse (especially between men) repulsive. And that, following Kass's logic, can be taken as a sign that homosexuality is contrary to human nature and perhaps also intrinsically wrong.[14]

As any number of critics have pointed out in response to Kass, "yuck" is a pretty weak basis on which to build an argument about human nature. Not only do the things that disgust human beings change dramatically over time, but our negative reactions also seem to be as much a product of historically contingent ignorance and prejudice as they are an expression of natural aversion. Defenders of anti-miscegenation laws, once described as a bulwark against the transgression of "natural" boundaries, also pointed to widely felt disgust among whites at the thought of interracial dating, marriage, and sexual intercourse. And yet here we are a few decades later, and most if not all of that disgust has disappeared, showing that it wasn't rooted in human nature at all—except, perhaps, in the sense that it might be natural for human beings to fear changes in established norms, practices, and beliefs.

That brings us to a final cluster of traditionalist arguments, all of them involving the claim that we should fear the social consequences of legalizing same-sex marriage. Traditionalists insist, first of all, that we should fear change, both in general and in the particular case of changing marriage laws to permit same-sex marriage. The general case against change amounts to the assertion that it tends to make things worse, since civilization is primarily held together with the glue of received custom. Without customary limits to channel, direct, and order our actions, human beings will behave like beasts, or worse, and so we tinker with and change received customs at our peril.

The generalized fear of change is an age-old human response to the world, and as such it has a certain dignity, especially in the modern age, when the pace and dynamism of our lives often leaves us feeling dizzy and disoriented. But does history really teach us that change always (or even often) leads to disaster? That sounds far too bleak. Yes, old customs die out, beliefs once held true begin to seem quaint and sometimes indefensible. But new ways evolve, new beliefs arise to take the place of those that no longer bind us, and the transformation is never absolute, or absolutely negative, because the natural tendencies and inclinations that underlie our customs ensure that change is accompanied by continuities on a deeper level.

Traditionalists cannot rely solely on a generalized fear of change to justify imposing their morality of ultimate ends on society as whole. They must demonstrate that in the particular case of changing marriage law to allow homosexuals to marry will have horrendous consequences—that ordinary Americans have well-founded reasons to fear that permitting same-sex marriage will lead traditional, heterosexual marriage, a bedrock institution of civilization, to collapse. And that's a tall order. Because there can be no empirical evidence in favor of (or against) a prospective argument like this one, traditionalists usually invoke a slippery slope to make their case, maintaining that once marriage is no longer viewed by our society as a whole as having a fixed character authored by God or nature, it will cease to be treated as binding on individuals, who will marry and divorce as easily and as often as their desires dictate, leaving suffering children behind to fend for themselves in the wreckage.

Yet traditionalists are making this argument far too late. It's been a very long time since our society as a whole believed marriage to have a fixed character authored by God or nature. One can lament this change. One can even argue that it has contributed in important ways to the rise of the morality of rights in relation to marriage, the liberalization of marital laws, and a subsequent spike in rates of divorce (which appear to have peaked in the late 1970s and early 1980s and have been declining ever since). But the change happened decades ago, its aftermath is now our settled custom, and though the demand for same-sex marriage might have been unthinkable before the change, it is hard to see how giving in to that demand will make much of a difference at this point. A majority of Americans marry. Somewhere between one-third and one-half of those marriages end in divorce—many of them having been filed under democratically enacted "no-fault divorce" statutes that permit either party to dissolve the union without having to show cause—and there is no reason to believe that these numbers will change substantially one way or the other once homosexuals (who make up a mere 4 percent of the American population) are granted the right to form (and dissolve) marital unions of their own.

Some traditionalists are aware of the problem. But instead of resigning themselves to the inevitability of gay marriage, they have chosen to take several steps further to the right, to make a far more radical critique of contemporary American life. Far from fixating on the narrow issue of same-sex marriage and its supposedly apocalyptic consequences, these so-called paleoconservatives denounce a much broader range of American institutions and customs, including the ideology of rights, the free market ideal, and the culture of individual choice that they believe has brought the nation to the brink of moral and spiritual collapse, with the demand for same-sex marriage just the latest sign of catastrophe. What we have to fear, they claim, is not a future in which same-sex marriage has been legalized and accepted, but rather the present as it is, what we have already become—namely, a culture in which traditional marriage and the age-old morality of ultimate ends with which it is intertwined can be placed on the defensive by homosexual activists proudly demanding their "right" to marry. Many of these paleocons believe the fight against same-sex marriage is a lost cause so long as its opponents fail to challenge the morality of rights that dominates the nation's public life and makes such demands sound reasonable or at least plausible to many Americans. In its place, as the only alternative to the United States falling further and further into decadence, they propose a nationwide recovery of a unified morality of ultimate ends and our collective obedience to an authority to enforce it.[15]

On two crucially important matters at least, the paleoconservatives are quite correct: the logic of the morality of rights makes it almost certain that same-sex marriage will eventually be publicly accepted throughout the United States, and the only way to prevent this outcome would be for the country as a whole (or something quite close to the country as a whole) to revert to the traditionalist morality of ultimate ends that prevailed in sexual matters until roughly fifty years ago.[16] Both claims should give liberals comfort, since short of a nationally experienced divine revelation, there is no chance at all of such a radical change coming to pass. Sexual traditionalism will persist in parts of the nation, but the days when it defined the nation as a whole are long gone and show no sign of returning.

Where liberals must break from the paleocons is of course in their bleak assessment of the American present and future—an assessment that flows from their tendency, which they share with other traditionalists, to portray the liberal morality of rights as a morality of ultimate ends that aims to stamp out contrary moral points of view. One reason why traditionalists view their situation in such stark terms is that they are convinced that public moralities are always moralities of ultimate ends: either America as a whole is defined by authoritarian sexual traditionalism or else America as a whole is defined by antinomian sexual liberation. There is no middle position. The liberal outlook, which is passionately committed to the middle position, is very different. It would permit homosexuals to marry, but it would also permit individuals and groups within civil society to organize their lives, if they so choose, around a morality of ends that rejects same-sex marriage. Liberalism is dedicated not to the creation of a homogeneously hedonistic society but rather to the perpetuation of a *pluralistic* society containing Provo as well as Provincetown, Lancaster as well as the Castro district.

Traditionalists rightly worry that state recognition of same-sex marriages will lead to a situation in which antidiscrimination statutes are invoked to curtail religious freedom. Opponents of same-sex marriage paint a wide range of nightmare scenarios. Some imagine clergy and religious communities being forced to solemnize same-sex marriages. Others claim that preaching against homosexuality could be prosecuted under hate crime statutes. Still others envision hospitals and universities affiliated with traditionalist religious institutions running into legal trouble for staying true to their principles and beliefs by refusing to recognize the marriages of same-sex couples.[17] Finally, many traditionalists foresee a future in which the nation's public schools treat the history of discrimination against homosexuals and their eventual acceptance into the mainstream of American life as perfectly analogous to the story of racial discrimination and the triumph of the movement for black civil rights. In that case, the liberal state would be actively working to undermine the sexual morality that traditionalists wish to pass on to their children.

Some would no doubt say that this is precisely what the liberal state should be doing, since it has as much of an interest in weakening homophobia as it has in weakening racism. But this fails to acknowledge the very different roles of race and gender in the Abrahamic religious traditions. While various religious texts have been used to justify racism and slavery over the centuries, these texts do not command adherents to adopt these practices in the way that they appear to command obedience to a series of strict teachings about gender roles and sexual propriety. This is to say that the attempt to use the public schools to stamp out homophobia is a far more profound challenge to the integrity of traditionalist religious beliefs than is the effort to drive out racism. If liberals want to avoid provoking a mass exodus of religious traditionalists from the public schools (and they should certainly want to avoid it), they must tread very cautiously in these matters, restraining the urge to educate traditionalists away from their deeply held religious convictions.[18]

But they must also go further, taking concrete, legal steps to guarantee that the religious freedom of traditionalists will be recognized and protected in a society that also recognizes and protects the political rights of homosexuals. This is the right thing to do—and not only because liberalism stands or falls by its willingness to defend freedom, even the freedom of those who devote themselves to moralities of ultimate ends that conflict with liberal ideals and aspirations. It is also the right thing to do because traditionalist beliefs really will be subjected to increasing, unprecedented legal pressure as homosexuality moves deeper and deeper into the mainstream of American life. This is the opinion not just of sometimes overly fearful traditionalists themselves but also of a wide range of legal scholars and journalists.

Liberals need to build on what states such as Connecticut and New Hampshire have already begun to do: include passages or amendments in same-sex-marriage legislation that explicitly define and protect the religious freedom of sexual traditionalists. This doesn't mean that traditionalists should get their way on every matter; the law traditionally limits claims to religious freedom when members of a religious community provide services outside their faith tradition (like adoption or hospital care) or enter the commercial marketplace (by, say, leasing a catering hall for wedding receptions). In such cases, religious traditionalists might be forced to recognize the legal validity of same-sex marriages (while presumably continuing to judge them morally and spiritually null and void). But on the all-important matter of religious freedom (in both speech and practice), liberals need to write laws and regulations in such a way that they unambiguously protect the right of traditionalists to preach their beliefs about the evils of homosexuality and pass those beliefs on to their children. By the same token, traditionalists should recognize and appreciate that even though American society as a whole no longer affirms their morality of ultimate ends, they benefit enormously from the protections granted and preserved by rights-based liberal institutions and procedures.

3

Unlike same-sex marriage, which seems destined by the "full faith and credit" clause of the US Constitution to be fought out at the national level, abortion would have remained a state matter if it hadn't been nationalized by the *Roe v. Wade* decision of 1973. That sometimes leads a pro-choice writer to suggest that the reversal of *Roe* would turn out to be a boon for the pro-choice cause, taking the wind out of the sails of the religious right, grounding women's equality and self-possession in the democratic process instead of in a controversial court decision, and opening up the possibility of achieving something like an armistice on the central front in the nation's culture wars.[19] All of these positive outcomes would supposedly flow from the salutary effects of federalism. With *Roe* overturned and the issue deflected back to the states, we could expect before long the formation of a new status quo marked by diminished national conflict over abortion along with a wide variety of abortion regulations. A few states—most of them places where abortions are already quite difficult to procure because few if any doctors or clinics perform them—would likely ban the procedure, while most others would impose quite modest restrictions, with a few imposing none at all.[20] After a few years of flux and confusion, in other words, women in a post-*Roe* America would likely face much the same set of options they do today. Meanwhile, the tone of our civic life would be dramatically improved, as the divisive issues wrapped up with the culture wars fade from national prominence and allow for compromises at the local level through democratic deliberation and debate. This would be federalism's gift to liberalism, contributing in a decisive way to allowing a pluralistic society to live in a state of relative peace.

It sounds great. But it's exceedingly unlikely to happen—and not only because with the victory of pro-choice Barack Obama in 2008, the right's long-sought fifth conservative Supreme Court vote needed to overturn *Roe* seems more elusive than ever. In the unlikely event that *Roe* were overturned, the results would almost certainly be less sunny than this optimistic scenario predicts. Far from witnessing a diminishment of cultural animus, we could expect it to surge and splinter, with emboldened pro-lifers seeking to capitalize on their judicial victory by lobbying hard for restrictions in state legislatures around the country and pro-choice activists mobilizing on all fifty fronts to combat them. In short, returning the issue to the states would likely lead to the opposite of cultural conciliation.[21]

It is easy to understand why. Activists on both sides of the issue frame it in a way that leads to absolute, maximalist stances. Neither will settle for compromise—not now, and not in some post-*Roe* future. But the more important and mysterious question is why pro-choice and pro-life activists have committed themselves to such stark positions in the first place. For to think deeply and rigorously about abortion is to see that it is among the most thoroughly tragic issues in our public life. This is not a moral condemnation; it is a moral observation. A tragedy in the classical sense is a situation that pits two legitimate moral claims against each other in such a way that one or the other must be sacrificed, despite its legitimacy. That describes the dilemma of abortion exactly. Given current polarization on the issue, there may be no good reason to hope for the kind of settlement that seems within reach on same-sex marriage. But given the tragic moral reality of abortion, it may make sense to hope that a greater number of our fellow citizens can be made to see the wisdom of the liberal approach to navigating the treacherous waters surrounding the issue.

The strongest—and most genuinely liberal—version of the pro-choice position builds on the tragic character of the choice faced by a woman who learns of an unwanted pregnancy: her own good and the good of the fetus lie on a collision course.[22] The woman's moral status is clear, or should be clear, to everyone. She is a person possessing rights to life and liberty, and so the liberal state is precluded from dictating what she does or does not do with her body. The fetus's moral status, by contrast, is murkier. Some—orthodox Catholics and many other traditionalist religious believers—consider that status obvious. But many others do not—and their views are based on widely shared moral intuitions and cultural practices. Couples do not normally grieve for a miscarried fetus with anything like the intensity that they do for a child who dies after birth. Neither will most couples choose to bury a fetus that has failed to make it to term. It is likewise a firmly established custom to measure human age from the time of birth, not from the time of conception. In these and innumerable other ways, we testify to the significance of birth as a threshold separating distinct phases of life. At birth, we become full-fledged residents of the human world that is governed by morality and law; but prior to birth, we exist in a kind of antechamber to that world, not quite the rights-bearing individuals we will be once we fully commence our lives outside the womb.

Confronted by the lack of consensus about the moral status of the fetus and the fact that it resides within the body of a person whose rights are inviolable, the liberal state responds as it always strives to do in such cases—by adopting a position of procedural neutrality. The choice to abort a fetus in a particular case might be right or it might be wrong: the liberal state takes no position. Instead, it leaves the decision and the accompanying moral deliberation up to the individuals most closely involved in the choice: the pregnant woman, of course, but also her partner, her family, and her friends. Under a liberal legal regime, a woman can consider abortion to be cold-blooded murder at any stage of pregnancy or see nothing wrong with late-term abortions or stake out a position anywhere between these poles. Many pro-choice Americans, in fact, find themselves in the morally complicated position of Mario Cuomo, the former governor of New York, who often described himself as both passionately pro-choice and "personally opposed" to abortion—meaning that he supported the *legality* of abortion while also believing it to be *morally* wrong to counsel someone to choose an abortion. The important thing for such defenders of abortion rights is that the morally fraught deliberation and choice be made free of political coercion; a woman and her doctor should never need to worry about being investigated, arrested, tried, and jailed for terminating a pregnancy. Reduced to the slogan we examined above in the context of same-sex marriage, the liberal position can summarized as: "Oppose abortion? Don't have one!"

This is the strongest version of the pro-choice argument because it is the most responsive to the tragic moral complexities involved in the issue. But precisely because of its nuanced insistence on drawing distinctions between moral and legal considerations, the liberal position is vulnerable to a simple but powerful pro-life objection. In response to the liberal insistence that the decision about whether or not abortion is tantamount to murder should be left up to individual women, pro-lifers ask: is there any other situation in which the liberal state grants individuals the right to determine for themselves what does and what does not constitute murder? The answer, of course, is no. And that, for pro-lifers, is evidence that the liberal pro-choice position is very far from being neutral with regard to the moral status of the fetus—that it, in fact, tacitly presumes the fetus to be morally insignificant and its fate a matter of moral indifference.

Repeatedly faced with this kind of objection, some defenders of abortion rights have responded not by developing a more compelling version of the liberal argument but rather by retreating to a more radical (and less complicated) position—one that essentially concedes the pro-life point and seeks to appropriate it for the pro-choice cause. That is, pro-choice radicals attempt to ensure the perpetuation of abortion rights by forcefully denying the moral status of the fetus and treating the decision about whether to terminate a pregnancy as entirely a matter of the woman's desires, with no consideration of anyone else's good, including the fetus's or the father's. Consider, for example, the case of "Maggie," a twenty-two-year-old college senior profiled in an article published by the left-wing website AlterNet in the summer of 2009.[23] Maggie was pregnant and had "no intention of bringing a child into the world yet," so her friends threw an "abortion party" to raise money for the procedure. At the party Maggie's boyfriend supported her decision but also made it clear that he was expected to accept it no matter what. It was Maggie's body, after all, and so his opinion about whether or not she would carry the fetus to term was beside the point. She wanted an abortion, so she would get an abortion—no questions asked, no shame involved, no consideration of alternatives. Just a simple, morally irrelevant choice.

Such sentiments will offend some people and reassure others. Provided that they are expressed at the individual level, they are politically immaterial. Yet when they are transformed into a legal principle—as activist groups such as Planned Parenthood and NARAL Pro-Choice America sometimes do—they can become highly problematic. At the most practical, political level, such extreme views are counterproductive, sharply alienating the American majority that is both pro-choice and deeply troubled by the thought of women using their reproductive freedom to procure abortions—especially serial abortions—for frivolous reasons.[24] What counts as "frivolous"? It seems sensible to assume that for most people—repelled by the absolutism found on both sides of the abortion debate—it depends on the context. Before the sexual revolution of the 1960s and 1970s, contraception was often hard to come by, while a pregnancy out of wedlock in most cases led a woman to be socially stigmatized. Neither is true today. Women have more ways than ever to prevent unwanted pregnancies, as well as a greater range of socially acceptable options for dealing with one when it happens. That means, oddly enough, that the sexual liberation of the past few decades has helped to create an environment in which there are now somewhat fewer situations than there once were in which choosing to have an abortion seems morally justifiable.

Another reason why increasing numbers of Americans may be coming to this conclusion is that progress in science and technology has been slowly strengthening the case for the humanity—and thus moral status—of the fetus. Unlike the thirteenth-century Thomas Aquinas, who believed the soul entered the fetus at "quickening" (the point, usually during the second trimester, when the mother feels the first stirrings of the fetus inside her), we now know that the fertilized egg becomes an embryo at some point between ten and fourteen days after conception—and that the embryo is genetically a distinct person, albeit an immature one.[25] The old debate about whether "life begins at conception" is thus now beside the point. The science of embryology clearly shows that personal identity begins roughly two weeks after conception—something brought home to most parents several weeks later when they get to see actual images of their baby in increasingly sophisticated ultrasound scans. To terminate a pregnancy after two weeks therefore terminates the life of a person at a very early stage of development. We can argue about the moral status of this person, but not about its status as a person.

That points to the most tragic (and increasingly common) situation of all—one in which a woman wants to have a child, recognizes that the fetus is a person, and yet learns through medical testing that it suffers from a severe handicap that will seriously impede its development and perhaps condemn it to a lifetime (often a drastically shortened lifetime) of extreme physical and emotional pain. In such cases, the good of the woman and the good of her child do not directly conflict as they do in the case of an unwanted pregnancy. On the contrary, the woman and those close to her must make a truly awful choice based on a judgment about her own good, the good of her family, and the (deeply uncertain) good of an unborn child with serious medical problems. What, dear reader, would you choose in such a situation? The honest answer, I suspect, is that you have no idea and could only know once you found yourself facing the heartbreaking decision yourself. What surely most of us can agree on is that none of the choices are good—and that making the choice would be rendered exponentially worse by forcing the woman (along with her family and her doctors) to factor into her decision the possibility of being arrested, tried, and punished by the state.

It should be clear that in highlighting the often wrenchingly tragic dimensions of abortion, my intention is not to make a case for the pro-life position. It is rather to show why defenders of reproductive rights should avoid seeking to protect those rights by (unconvincingly) treating abortion as a matter of moral or emotional indifference—as Maggie, her partner, and their friends are portrayed as doing at the "abortion party." The more compelling approach to defending wom-

en's freedom—more compelling because more attuned and responsive to the clashing, often irresolvable moral imperatives involved in
abortion—is the liberal one, which does not presume or require Maggie's boyfriend to go along passively with her decision to terminate
her pregnancy. A man can fiercely defend a woman's (public) right
to choose an abortion without state interference while also passionately trying to persuade his girlfriend (in private) to carry their (not
her) baby to term. In the end, she should be permitted to abort the
child if he fails to convince her, even if he continues to object. (Spou-
sal consent laws move the decision back into the public—legal and
political—sphere and thus will be rightly rejected by a liberal defender
of reproductive freedom.) But there might be personal consequences
from the dispute. The man might break up with his girlfriend over the
disagreement, just as she may break up with him. Or maybe they will
move past it as a couple. Whatever the outcome, the decision about
whether or not to abort will have been made where it should be—in
private, by those most closely involved and most deeply immersed in
the moral texture of the situation.

4

Opponents of legalized abortion like to portray themselves as the real
liberals in the debate over reproductive freedom, defending a morality of rights (the rights of the fetus) against its enemies. But what
about the pregnant woman? To judge from pro-life arguments, opponents of abortion have little interest in or even tolerance for the rights
and dignity of women *as women*—as opposed to their rights and dignity *as mothers*. In other words, pro-lifers superimpose a sexually traditionalist morality of ultimate ends—one that assumes a woman's
innate end or purpose is to give birth to and raise children—onto the
morality of rights it champions. This has the effect of minimizing, if

not eliminating, the moral conflict at the heart of the abortion issue. For a committed abortion opponent, there can be no such thing as a genuine clash between the good of a fetus and the good of the woman carrying a fetus. When a woman senses a tension between conflicting goods—or when she feels compelled by circumstances to terminate a pregnancy—it is a sign that something (feminist ideology, economic hardship, careerism, an unethical form of medical ethics, mental illness) has fundamentally distorted her perception of her natural instincts and inclinations, which in themselves could never lead her to view pregnancy as anything other than a blessing.

Abortion opponents thus go easy on themselves, making assumptions that simplify and obscure the tragic tensions at the heart of the issue. Are pro-lifers primarily out to protect the fetus's right to life? Or do they want to uphold and use state power to enforce a traditionalist morality of ultimate ends in which women always put motherhood ahead of other goods (or even refuse to see any pursuit besides motherhood as a good)? If they were mainly concerned with protecting the lives of fetuses, pro-lifers would presumably pursue numerous strategies in addition to seeking the reversal or narrowing of *Roe v. Wade.* They might fight to make birth control more widely available and support educational programs that advocate its use.[26] They might seek to fund quality, affordable child care so that women could more effectively balance motherhood and career rather than view them as antagonistic. But the pro-life movement does nothing of the sort.

The question is why. And the answer is that the groups that form the core of the pro-life movement—conservative Catholics, evangelical Protestants, and Mormons—are as committed to upholding and enforcing a traditionalist morality of gender roles as they are to the defense of fetal life. The movement has a stake in blurring the distinction between these very different and partially divergent goals, which is one important reason why it cannot support policies that encourage the use of birth control or make it easier for mothers to work outside the home, even though such policies would likely do quite a lot to lower the abortion rate.

That's also why pro-lifers remain so fixated on overturning *Roe*. Yes, pro-lifers reject the 1973 decision because they think it decriminalizes the murder of an innocent and defenseless person. But for many of them, there is something even bigger at stake. *Roe* declared that the nation's Constitution—its fundamental law—is incompatible with the opinion that abortion is the murder of an innocent and defenseless person. The pro-life movement is as much a reaction to this declaration as it is a protest against a woman's right to choose an abortion. It is an expression, in other words, of identity politics—the spirited refusal of a group of Americans to accept that its views are constitutionally unacceptable. In effect, abortion opponents are saying to the Supreme Court: "This is my country, too, and so you are wrong to think that We the People affirm the right of a mother to murder her baby. We the People affirm no such thing."

There is no better way to galvanize a political movement than to ground it in group grievance, just as there is no better way to keep a political movement from splintering into squabbling factions than to downplay tensions in its agenda. The relentless focus on overturning *Roe* accomplishes both for the pro-life movement. What it doesn't do is reduce the number of abortions in the United States. Some of the roughly 40 percent of Americans who think abortion should be illegal in all or most cases are undoubtedly motivated by identity politics and the urge to use state power to get women to affirm a traditionalist morality of ultimate ends—and a few might actually relish the thought of throwing women and their doctors in jail.[27] But surely many others are primarily driven by the desire to lower the abortion rate. These more moderate critics of abortion should be receptive to evidence that the culturally reactionary pro-life movement has done virtually nothing over the past three decades to decrease the number of abortions in the United States. It should thus also be possible to persuade some of them that pro-choice politicians (such as Barack Obama) and religious leaders (such as evangelical Jim Wallis) are likely to make far more progress by addressing the social and economic factors that lead thousands of American women to choose to terminate their pregnancies every year.

There is no political or legal way out of the conundrum of abortion; the competing moral claims are simply too intractable. Something similar might be said more generally of the nation's sex wars, which look likely to remain a fixture of our cultural life for the foreseeable future. Still, good-faith efforts by supporters of abortion rights to encourage women to make different choices with their constitutionally protected freedom—efforts that will hopefully be expanded over the coming years to include federal programs that both promote the use of contraception and grant all women access to quality, affordable child care—could do a lot of good. Not only would they likely contribute in important ways to mitigating the stark moral trade-offs that lie at the heart of abortion; they might even help to convince greater numbers of Americans to favor the liberal position on the political regulation—or rather, deregulation—of sex.

VI

The Intolerance
of the Freethinkers

I n the penultimate chapter of his bestselling book *The God Delusion*, biologist and world-renowned atheist Richard Dawkins presents his view of religious education, which he elaborates by way of an anecdote. Following a lecture in Dublin, he recalls, "I was asked what I thought about the widely publicized cases of sexual abuse by Catholic priests in Ireland. I replied that, horrible as sexual abuse no doubt was, the damage was arguably less than the long-term psychological damage inflicted by bringing the child up Catholic in the first place." Lest his readers misunderstand him, or dismiss this rather shocking statement as mere off-the-cuff hyperbole, Dawkins goes on to clarify his position. "I am persuaded," he explains, "that the phrase 'child abuse' is no exaggeration when used to describe what teachers and priests are doing to children whom they encourage to believe in something like the punishment of unshriven mortal sins in an eternal hell."[1]

Dawkins is hardly alone in holding such views. In his own book he quotes psychologist Jill Mytton on the similarities between sexual abuse and the "mental abuse" involved in raising a child to believe in biblical religion.[2] Another psychologist, Nicholas Humphrey, goes even further—insinuating in passages, which Dawkins quotes at length, that raising a child in a religious tradition, like other forms of child abuse, should be considered a crime punishable by the state. Children, according to Humphrey, possess the right "not to have their minds crippled by exposure to other people's bad ideas" or "addled by nonsense." Parents, meanwhile, no more have the right "to teach their children to believe in the literal truth of the Bible" or "to limit the horizon of their children's knowledge" or "to bring them up in an atmosphere of dogma and superstition" than they do "to knock their children's teeth out or lock them in a dungeon."[3] The implication of such statements is clear: Humphrey (and by extension Dawkins himself) would prefer to live in a world in which the government strictly regulated what parents are permitted to teach their children about God.

Why Dawkins refrains from openly advocating the forcible removal of children from the homes of religious parents is a mystery, for it follows directly from the character of the atheism he and his quoted authorities so forcefully espouse. And not only theirs. In recent years, the wholesale denunciation of religion has become something of a cottage industry in the United States. Author Sam Harris has written two bestsellers animated by the conviction that the Bible and Koran "contain mountains of life-destroying gibberish."[4] Comedian and talk-show host Bill Maher ridiculed piety in his documentary *Religulous*—a film that treated religious belief as a "neurological disorder." And then there is the polemicist Christopher Hitchens, whose manifesto *God Is Not Great* culminates in a call for humanity to treat religion as the "enemy," and to "prepare to fight it." According to Hitchens, such spiritual militancy is our only hope of escaping "the gnarled hands which reach out to drag us back to the catacombs and the reeking altars and the guilty pleasures of subjection and abjection."[5]

Journalists have dubbed this combative style of challenging religious belief "the new atheism." To the extent that the appellation is meant to highlight the novelty of virulently antireligious ideas finding a mass audience in the United States, it is certainly fitting. But as a description of the style of unbelief itself, it demonstrates a striking lack of historical awareness. That's because the "new atheism" is not particularly new. It belongs to an intellectual genealogy stretching back over two hundred years, to a moment in the late eighteenth century when atheist thought split into two traditions, with the new branch repudiating the cautious and nuanced tone of previous styles of atheism. Whereas atheists before and since the split have usually gone beyond expressions of theological skepticism to explore the complicated questions and concerns that arise when one sets out to live a life without God, members of the new *ideological* branch of atheism tend to be indifferent to such issues and primarily motivated by an intolerant contempt for the personal beliefs of others.

Today's bellicose atheists are the latest representatives of the ideological offshoot of the broader atheist tradition. And it is not surprising that they have found a sizeable audience for the contemporary repackaging of their centuries-old ideas. To citizens frightened by the faith-based conservatism of religious traditionalists or the theological fanaticism of Osama bin Laden—or both—the scalding language of Dawkins, Harris, Maher, and Hitchens sounds refreshing, apt, and bold. But the intellectual lineage to which these authors belong should in fact give pause to those on the liberal side of the culture wars. Among other problems, it isn't a liberal tradition at all.

1

Atheism—the denial of the existence of personal, providential gods who intervene in human lives, hear and answer prayers, and reward the righteous and punish the wicked—has been around for a very long time, almost as long as the belief that such gods exist. But a distinctly ideological form of atheism did not fully flower until the late eighteenth century, building on and radicalizing intellectual trends that began more than a century earlier, in mid-seventeenth-century Europe. Shocked by the senseless bloodshed of the religious civil wars that pitted groups of Roman Catholics against various Protestant factions throughout the continent, skeptics revived several forms of ancient doubt in the hope of reforming the cultures of Western civilization—of rendering them more moderate and civil, less intolerant and cruel. Thomas Hobbes, to take one influential example, developed a new science of humanity and politics to solve problems of government in a world torn between competing transcendent allegiances. Baruch Spinoza, meanwhile, contributed to the edification of the European mind by constructing an elaborate (and idiosyncratic) philosophical system that combined rigorous biblical criticism with a rationalist theology of a radically impersonal God. Still others, like Pierre Bayle, popularized philosophical skepticism in the hope that it might moderate the mores of modern men and women. What these thinkers shared was relative optimism about the possibility of religious doubt playing a positive practical role in the world.

None of these writers sought to create a godless society. Whatever the personal views of such writers as Hobbes, Spinoza, and Bayle—not to mention their American philosophical cousins James Madison and Thomas Jefferson—they publicly promoted not atheism but liberal Judaism and Christianity. This was the case even in France, where eighteenth-century authors such as Baron d'Holbach, Claude Adrien Helvétius, and the Marquis de Condorcet began confidently to dismiss religion in tones familiar to us from the modern-day pronouncements of such scientifically minded skeptics as Sigmund Freud, Albert Einstein, Carl Sagan, and Steven Weinberg.[6] Although these French writers firmly rejected faith in a personal, providential God, they directed their harshest criticisms at the Catholic Church, not at God or religion in general.

It was not until the final years of the eighteenth century, in the late, fanatical phases of the French Revolution, that a wholly politicized—or ideological—form of atheism fully emerged. Convinced that the religious toleration guaranteed in the 1789 Declaration of the Rights of Man and Citizen permitted ignorance to thrive in the revolutionary republic, antireligious crusaders such as Jacques Hébert sought nothing less than to de-Christianize France. Hébert's pamphlets make for shocking reading, even today. The content of one is nicely captured by its title: "Fuck the Pope." Another recounts an argument with a priest—a "fucking liar"—that ends in violence ("He wanted to respond to me, but in my anger I gave him the hardest fucking slap that the fucking face of a rascal ever received"). A third laments that because there "aren't enough torturers in the world" to take care of all the "buggers worthy of the wheel," revolutionary France would have to make do with the guillotine.[7]

These pamphlets were written in 1790. Over the next several years, the furious indignation that inspired them would come to political power in Paris, with singularly unhappy results. Hébert and his allies Jacques-Claude Bernard and Pierre-Gaspard Chaumette encouraged their supporters (called Hébertists) to ransack and desecrate churches and cathedrals, transforming them through iconoclastic violence into "Temples of Reason." At first clergy were deported, then public and even private worship was outlawed. Finally, a law enacted on October

21, 1793, made all priests, as well as anyone suspected of harboring one, subject to death on sight.

The leaders of the Cult of Reason were eventually guillotined, consumed by the very brutality they had helped to unleash. Yet their brand of atheism lived on in European politics. Unlike their seventeenth- and eighteenth-century forerunners, who tended to examine religious claims in a spirit of skepticism and doubt, the new ideological atheists typically dismissed the possibility of God with strident certainty. This confidence also contributed to their characteristic indifference to exploring—or even acknowledging—the personal and social challenges that can follow from the rejection of religion. Ideological atheists have thus tended to be unshakably convinced of both the possibility and goodness of spreading god-lessness to every corner of the globe—and they have often been willing and eager to use state power to accomplish this extraordinarily ambitious goal.

Ideological atheism received its classic theoretical justification in the writings of Auguste Comte, Ludwig Feuerbach, and Karl Marx. Marx's mode of argumentation proved to be especially influential. In an important essay from 1843, Marx distinguished between two forms of emancipation. On the one hand, liberal democracy produces *political* emancipation by privatizing religion and institutionalizing toleration of religious differences. But, as Marx noted, this form of emancipation is perfectly compatible with "the *immense majority* of people continu[ing] to be religious."[8] To make his case, Marx pointed out that in the United States, a country that "has attained full political emancipation," religion "not only continues to *exist* but is *fresh* and *vigorous*."[9] Mere political emancipation therefore leaves human beings enslaved to the falsehoods of faith, since it "does not abolish, and does not even strive to abolish, man's *real* religiosity."[10] And that is a problem. Marx therefore concludes that "to be finally and completely emancipated from religion," a more radical form of liberation, which he calls *human* emancipation, is necessary.[11]

As it would be with his later call for the overthrow of capitalism, Marx's writing became opaquely abstract when he attempted to discuss how to eliminate religion from the world. In the first section of his 1843 essay, for example, the reader learns that "human emancipation will only be complete when the real, individual man has absorbed into himself the abstract citizen" and when "he has become a *species-being*."[12] Does this mean that liberal citizens ought merely to do a better job of internalizing the Declaration of the Rights of Man and Citizen? Or is it a call for an atheist state to confiscate church property, jail clergymen, and execute those who stubbornly persist in their piety? It is impossible to say.

The second section of Marx's essay, which focused on the specific problem of the persistence of Jews in the modern state, raised several troubling questions—and not only because Marx trafficked in blatant anti-Semitism, describing Jews as "hucksters" who worship the worldly god of money.[13] Equally alarming was his suggestion that society abolish "the empirical essence of Judaism," meaning "hucksterism and its conditions," which would lead in turn to "the Jew" becoming "*impossible*."[14] Once again the concrete meaning of these ominous statements is somewhat obscure, but the intent of Marx's ideological atheism is plain: the full liberation of humanity from the dead weight of religion requires the abolition of Judaism.

That the first ideological atheists, from Hébert to Marx, were found on the European left is historically interesting but theoretically irrelevant; Ernst Jünger, Werner Sombart, Hans Freyer, and many other figures of the far right would soon join them in pronouncing the absurdity of traditional religious belief.[15] What the far left and right shared, besides a hatred of religion, was an irrepressible loathing for liberalism, which permits citizens to continue worshipping their gods in peace, protected by state power from persecution. For Europe's ideological atheists, this was an indefensible concession to superstition and prejudice.

2

Until recently, ideological atheism hardly played any cultural role in the United States, where intellectuals and other elites have tended to refrain from challenging popularly held religious convictions too forcefully. Many of the constitutional framers, for example, subscribed to deism—the belief that the universe and its natural laws were created by a personal God who has ceased to play a providential role in human life or history. In this as in so many other ways, the founders marked a path that American critics of religion would take again and again: denouncing the foolishness of this or that religious institution while simultaneously affirming one of several heterodox forms of religious belief. In most cases, the form of belief—whether deism, Unitarianism, pantheism, or John Dewey's religion of democratic "common faith"—has been perfectly compatible with liberal government.

There have of course been exceptions to this American consensus. The pragmatist philosopher Sidney Hook, for example, cultivated a tolerant form of atheism. In a 1950 essay for *Partisan Review*, Hook asserted that "as a set of cognitive beliefs, religious doctrines constitute a speculative hypothesis of an extremely low order of probability," while also conceding that, for many, faith in God served as "a source of innocent joy, a way of overcoming cosmic loneliness." As long as these comforting religious views were "conceived in personal terms" and did not take "authoritarian institutional form," Hook maintained, they should "fall in an area of choice in which rational criticism may be suspended."[16]

Those few in the American past who adhered to ideological atheism have naturally taken a much less accommodating view. Some,
like the Russian American anarchist Emma Goldman, imported their
strident "negation of gods" directly from European sources. Others,
like the nineteenth-century intellectual Robert Ingersoll and Planned
Parenthood founder Margaret Sanger, did not so much emulate Europeans as end up in a similar position by following through indepen-
dently on the logic of antireligious ideas and combining them with
a typically American optimism about the morally salutary consequences of scientific progress.[17]

Then there was the activist Madalyn Murray O'Hair, who leapt to
prominence in the 1960s by advocating a uniquely vulgar and hate-
filled version of ideological atheism. In her notorious 1965 interview
with *Playboy* magazine, Murray O'Hair expressed bald-faced contempt
for religion and those who believe in it.[18] Religion, she claimed, "is a
crutch, and only the crippled need crutches." To be sure, she denied
that people should be compelled by the state not to practice their faith
or "stripped of their right to the insanity of belief in God." Yet she also
condemned religion for inflicting "psychic damage" on "generations
of children who might have grown up into healthy, happy, productive,
zestful human beings but for the burden of antisexual fear and guilt
ingrained in them by the church." Such charges—combined with the
extremism of her judgment that Christianity has never "contributed
anything to anybody, anyplace, at any time"—lead one to wonder why
she believed religion should be tolerated at all.

Back in the mid-sixties, Murray O'Hair's fanatical hostility to faith
held little mainstream appeal. Only now, during the past few years,
have authors and entertainers espousing a similarly ferocious style
of ideological atheism attracted widespread interest, most likely in
reaction to the rise of militant Islam abroad and the Christian right
at home. With fervent believers sowing political instability and some-

times resorting to violence around the world, it makes sense that secular citizens would gravitate to the so-called new atheists. In the syncretic writings of Harris, Dawkins, and Hitchens, readers find useful compendia of arguments against God from throughout history. One chapter summarizes the findings of modern biblical scholarship and archeology, another rehearses classic philosophical objections to belief in divine revelation, yet another makes the case for the scientific method and ridicules the dogmas and doctrines of established churches. Little of it is original, but most of it is clearly and passionately presented in lively, often electrifying prose.[19]

What makes these figures ideological atheists is the intensity of their passionate hatred for religion in all of its forms, as well as for those who believe in it. Yet there are important differences between the writers when it comes to the practical consequences of their godlessness. At one end of the spectrum is Christopher Hitchens, who works to reproduce Murray O'Hair's attempted synthesis of antireligious zealotry with an affirmation of religious freedom. Hitchens rails indiscriminately against religion on every page of *God Is Not Great*—declaring (in italics no less) that *"religion poisons everything,"* denouncing the Christian Bible as "spiritualist drivel" and "deranged science fiction," dismissing the Hebrew Bible as the scribblings of "provincial yokels," describing "people of faith" as "planning your and my destruction, and the destruction of all . . . hard-won human attainments"—all the while insisting that he would not prohibit religion "even if I thought I could."[20] Readers will have to take him at his word.

Richard Dawkins and Sam Harris, by contrast, are much less scrupulous in rendering their judgments. Or perhaps they are more willing to own up to the political implications of their antireligious ire. Although Dawkins never explicitly calls for the persecution of religion, he goes to great lengths (as we have seen) to demonstrate that

religious education is a form of child abuse, which is of course to suggest it is a crime deserving of punishment by the state. Harris, for his
part, goes even further—to denounce "the very ideal of religious tolerance." In his view, the conviction that "every human being should
be free to believe whatever he wants about God" is, very simply, "one
of the principal forces driving us toward the abyss."[21]

What Harris means by this remarkable statement becomes abundantly clear in the course of his book *The End of Faith*. Harris informs
us in his acknowledgments that he began writing on September 12,
2001, during the nation's "collective grief and stupefaction" following
the terrorist attacks of the previous day.[22] One thus might suppose
that his rejection of toleration is meant to apply merely to religious
extremists—to those believers whose intense piety threatens public
safety and human life in free societies everywhere. In that case, Harris would be offering a kind of corollary to the Bush administration's
post-9/11 policies regarding the treatment of terrorist suspects—
asserting, in effect, that the threat to the nation by religious fanatics
is so great that the government must temporarily break from constitutional norms by taking extraordinary (and temporary) actions in
its self-defense. Harris would then be making the controversial but
perfectly defensible argument that a tolerant society need not—and
ought not—extend toleration to those who seek its destruction.

But this is not at all—or not merely—what Harris has in mind. This
becomes obvious almost immediately after his condemnation of toleration, when he turns his critical attention not to religious extremists
but to religious moderates. A moderate believer, he claims, is "nothing more than a failed fundamentalist"—that is, someone who knows
enough about science to reject the most absurd passages of Scripture
but who arbitrarily decides to affirm the truth of other passages that
appeal to him on subjective moral or spiritual grounds. This, according to Harris, is a betrayal of "faith and reason equally." In his view,

all believers should be fundamentalists who insist that scriptural texts are "perfect in all their parts," while all rational human beings ought to be thoroughgoing atheists who reject religion root and branch. By blurring these bright lines, moderates do nothing to lead us "out of the wilderness" and contribute quite a lot to relaxing our standards of truth and knowledge, which are our only effective weapon against the forces of darkness.[23] It is thus the moderate believers who pose the greater threat to our society—and thus they, too, should not be tolerated.

Perhaps we should be grateful to Harris for following through so consistently on his convictions. One wonders, in fact, if any of the new atheists would dissent from Harris's frontal assault on the ideal of religious toleration.[24] After all, if "faith is an evil" that "can be very very dangerous," as Dawkins claims, then toleration may very well be a luxury we can no longer afford. If religion poisons *everything*, as Hitchens contends, then we had better be prepared to deal with it harshly. If our only options are to "grow up or die," as comedian Bill Maher quite seriously insists at the conclusion of his polemical documentary *Religulous* (over ominous music and images of mushroom clouds), then the time may very well have come for us to follow Harris's advice and command public schools to "announce the death of God" to their students, thereby ending the liberal state's theological neutrality, repealing the First Amendment's guarantee of religious free exercise, and inaugurating a time of state-sponsored antagonism toward the religious beliefs of American citizens.[25]

3

The ideological atheism of Harris, Dawkins, Hitchens, and Maher is an intolerant, proselytizing faith, out to rack up conversions. But so what? Religious believers of every stripe are free to knock on doors—

and to write books, articles, and ad copy, not to mention to broadcast their opinions on radio, television and the Internet—all in an effort to get their fellow citizens to abandon the error of their ways and follow the Truth. Shouldn't atheists be permitted to do something similar by producing books and films that might insult or offend believers? Of course. But conceding that the new atheists have a right to say what they do is quite a different thing from endorsing what they say and how they say it. On the matter of substance, the new atheists deserve to be roundly criticized for flirting with—and even actively embracing and publicly propagating—political and intellectual illiberalism.

The political illiberalism of the new atheists is plain for all to see. Liberals from the nation's founding to today have tended to defend secular *politics* while allowing (and sometimes even encouraging) society to remain permeated by various forms of religiosity. On this Marx was absolutely correct: political liberalism merely privatizes religion, it doesn't eliminate it. The new atheists, on the other hand, have the much more radical goal of producing a secular *society*—a society in which the American people, as a whole and individually, have abandoned religion. That, in itself, isn't enough to make the new atheists politically illiberal. If they steadfastly limited themselves to making arguments against religion and persuading their readers one at a time through argument and rhetoric, then they would merely be missionaries for godlessness using their liberal freedom to generate converts to their cause. Hitchens struggles to maintain this posture throughout much of *God Is Not Great*. Harris and Dawkins, however, end up in a more disturbing position, advocating (or in Dawkins's case, strongly implying that he endorses) the use of state power to help bring about a thoroughly atheistic society.

The intellectual illiberalism of the new atheists is far more pervasive in their thinking, though it is perhaps harder for us to detect. That's because we've come to think of liberalism entirely in political

terms—as a philosophy of limited government that strives for neutrality in matters of religion.[26] But political liberalism derives, at its
deepest level, from an older understanding of liberalism—as a habit
of mind connected to the classical virtue of liberality, which meant
generosity and openness. This notion of liberalism underlies the
idea of the "liberal arts" as a curriculum that imparts general knowledge of the humanities and at its best instills a sense of humility by
opening the student to the full range of human experience, thinking,
and feeling. It is liberalism in this high-minded sense that the long,
multifaceted humanistic tradition of atheism managed to affirm and
exemplify—and that the new atheists reject.

4

From the time of atheism's earliest origins in ancient Greece, religious skeptics have looked to natural causes to explain phenomena
that most of their fellow citizens considered to be the work of divine
agents. Socrates was portrayed as one of these atheists in Aristo-
phanes' *The Clouds*—an accusation that likely contributed to him
being sentenced to death for the capital crimes of impiety and cor-
rupting the youth of Athens. Socrates may be the most celebrated
martyr to atheism, but many other philosophers and scientists,
before and since, have faced political persecution for their insistence
on subjecting the religious beliefs and practices of their communities to rigorous, skeptical scrutiny. Anaxagoras, Protagoras, Aristotle,
Avicenna, Averroes, Descartes, Spinoza, Rousseau, and Kant are just
a few of the writers who faced such hostility, some of it violent. Fear of
persecution led many unbelievers to express their views with a tenta-
tiveness quite unlike the bold, often deliberately provocative declarations of today's ideological atheists, who write and think in conditions
of political freedom.

But the cautious intellectual style of premodern atheists did not derive entirely from a concern with self-preservation. It also flowed from the character of their skepticism. Philosophers have always been capable of demolishing this or that claim on behalf of piety—of undermining the veracity of evidence presented in favor of particular gods. But what about the religious impulse in general? Can it be overcome? By everyone? Or only by a few? What are its psychological and social roots? Assuming emancipation from religion is possible at least for some, is it good? Good for the emancipated individual himself? What about for an emancipated society? Would such an atheistic society thrive? Go on as if nothing had changed? Or would it collapse into nihilistic immorality and misery? Unlike the strident ideological atheists of today, who tend to denounce faith in all of its forms and view liberation from religious belief as an unambiguous good for all human beings in all times and places, history's nonideological atheists have reached a wide range of answers to these questions. Interestingly, these answers have often pointed in the direction of modesty and restraint, convincing them that it would be foolish to act as missionaries for godlessness.

Consider the paradigmatic case of Socrates, the philosopher whose relentless questioning of his fellow citizens has inspired skeptics throughout the ages. The conversations recorded (and presumably embellished) in the dialogues of his student Plato show us a Socrates unflinchingly devoted to the cause of subjecting received opinions about virtually every facet of morality and religion to dialectical examination, criticism, and refinement. Yet Plato also portrays a Socrates governed by a spirit of humility. Whereas his fellow citizens boasted about their own wisdom (while proving to be incapable of defending their opinions about justice, the gods, and many other crucially important matters), Plato's teacher was motivated above all by doubt about his own wisdom—or rather, by the conviction that his wisdom consisted in knowing the limits of his own knowledge.[27] Socrates was so committed to leading a life in pursuit of the knowledge he lacked that he famously preferred to accept a death sentence to living out the remainder of his days in conformity to a lesser penalty that would have required him to cease interrogating the beliefs of his fellow Athenians.[28]

Yet, despite their compelling defense of the philosophic way of life, there is little evidence that Socrates or Plato thought skeptical inquiry would ever be widely accepted, let alone commonly practiced. In the famous allegory in Book VII of Plato's *Republic*, Socrates insists that the overwhelming majority of human beings live their lives chained to the floor of a cave, gazing at shadow images that they ignorantly mistake for reality. Philosophers are those exceedingly rare individuals who come to doubt reigning opinions about the shadows and seek to replace those opinions with knowledge. In doing so, they liberate themselves from their confinement in the cave and ultimately ascend to the outside world, leaving behind the shadowy, imperfect goods that prevail underground in favor of a life bathed in the light of the sun, which in Plato's allegory represents the eternal, unchanging Idea of the Good.

Rarely has the life of doubt been presented with such sublimity—or as residing atop such a rigid hierarchy. While the vast run of humanity dogmatically affirms the *seeming* truth and goodness of various unexamined moral and religious opinions, the rarest human type (the philosopher) gets to enjoy the rich and enduring rewards that flow from the contemplation of what *is* true and good. Plato appears to have believed, in other words, that skeptical inquiry is its own reward—but also that it is a reward that very few human beings are capable of enjoying. He would thus likely have considered any attempt to spread philosophical skepticism among the nonphilosophical multitude a futile pursuit as well as a dangerous one, as the fate of his beloved teacher so vividly demonstrates.

Plato's exalted account of Socratic inquiry was taken up and developed in very different ways by numerous philosophical schools in the ancient world. Some, like Aristotle and Plotinus, took off from Plato's oracular pronouncements about the Idea of the Good to develop elaborate, often highly abstruse rational theologies about an "unmoved mover" or the mystical emanations of the "One." These speculative accounts of an impersonal, non-providential divine "mind" have sometimes been described (somewhat facetiously) as "gods of the philosophers" to distinguish them from the personal, providential God revealed in the Hebrew and Christian Bibles. The authors of these ornate rationalist systems certainly never expected their distinctly unconsoling metaphysical teachings to be disseminated among and adopted by non-philosophers.

Other thinkers, like Carneades and Sextus Empiricus, moved in a more consistently skeptical direction. Following the example of Socrates' open-ended questioning and emphasizing the limits of reason, these thinkers maintained that rational reflection terminates in doubt and uncertainty. When it came to metaphysics and theology, they tended to hold that wisdom consists in accepting that, in the words of their eighteenth-century descendant David Hume, "the whole is a riddle, an enigma, an inexplicable mystery."[29] Many in this tradition have also maintained that suspension of judgment about metaphysical questions can produce a mild but enduring peace of mind—though only for the few who are capable of it.[30]

And then there is Epicureanism, the ancient philosophical school that affirmed atomistic materialism, explicitly denied the existence of providential gods, and maintained that pleasure is the highest human good (and pain the greatest evil). Epicurus and his followers believed that if human beings could only overcome their ignorance and fear—above all, their fear of divine retribution in an imaginary afterlife—they would begin to experience the tranquility that comes from an absence of pain and the modest enjoyment of physical and intellectual pleasure. (Epicurean hedonism was inextricably linked to moderation.) But the Epicureans also recognized that such tranquility is a rare achievement—rare because most human beings long for greater, more intense, longer-lasting goods than the ones that can be realistically hoped for in a disenchanted world. The overwhelming majority of men and women would rather persist in ignorance and fear, and suffer the pain that accompanies them, than accept the austerity of the Epicurean teaching.[31]

The philosophical schools of antiquity thus varied greatly in their positive teachings, but they agreed about two crucially important matters. All of them denied the existence of personal, providential gods, and all of them doubted the willingness or ability of most human beings to accept this denial. Their doubts had many sources. Some of them flowed from unexamined aristocratic assumptions about natural hierarchy. Just as men were held to be superior to women and free individuals to slaves, so the philosophic wise man was thought to possess an exceedingly rare set of virtues that elevated him by nature above the rest of humanity. But aristocratic prejudice was not the only basis for ancient doubts about the popular acceptance of atheism. Engaging in a dialectical examination of moral and religious opinions really did require an unusually high degree of intelligence and stamina, just as accepting the harsh reality of life in a godless world demanded greater courage and composure than most men and women possessed. The result was the distinctively ancient philosophical position that although the truth is both beautiful and good, it can be recognized and appreciated as such only by the few whose intellectual and moral virtues render them capable of discovering and enduring it.

Atheists of later eras have often been similarly pessimistic about the possibility and goodness of spreading godlessness, though this pessimism usually flowed from different considerations. Voltaire's objection to the providential God of the Bible, for example, is at bottom an objection rooted in biblical morality and anthropology. Writing in response to the devastating Lisbon earthquake of 1755, in which tens of thousands died (many of them in collapsed churches), Voltaire echoed the gospels—and anticipated the indignation of Ivan in Dostoevsky's *Brothers Karamazov*—by describing human life as a vale of tears: "The whole world in every member groans: / All born for torment and for mutual death." Recoiling from this bloody tableau, humanity cries out to the heavens for consolation—for a hand to wipe away every tear and redeem us from our sorrows and suffering.

Unlike the imaginary world of Scripture, the real world—a world in which "evil stalks the land"—knows no such consolation. The God defined by theologians as infinitely powerful and good appears to do nothing to prevent our pain, and He seems to respond to our agony with perfect silence, leaving mankind to wonder in bitter solitude, "Why suffer we, then, under one so just?"[32] For Voltaire and many other moralistic atheists, the answer to this nagging question has been obvious and decisive: either God is less powerful and good than He is typically presumed to be, or else He does not exist—and all of our anguished cries are in vain, reverberating impotently throughout an indifferent universe, where they go forever unheard and unanswered. It is a sad and sobering possibility, which perhaps explains why those who have espoused it have rarely sought to proselytize in its name.

The same might be said for the tragic stoicism of such atheists as the writer Albert Camus and the poet Philip Larkin.[33] For Camus, in such works as *The Myth of Sisyphus*, the absence of God does not merely undermine human hopes for redemption, as it did for Voltaire; it also, and more ominously, threatens to render absurd every form of human striving, from the ambition to accomplish great deeds to the far more mundane activities of pursuing a career, raising a family, and even getting out of bed in the morning. This is why Camus devoted so much time to the question of suicide: when the longing for transcendent meaning—for a satisfying answer to the question of "why?"—confronts the "unreasonable silence of the world," the goodness of human life appears to dissolve and must be reconstructed from the ground up.[34]

What makes Camus a stoic is his conviction that such a reconstruction can only be undertaken on the basis of an admittedly absurd leap of faith that affirms the goodness of life despite its ultimate pointlessness. Sisyphus rolls his rock up the mountain, watches it roll back down to the bottom, and then begins the process again, in full knowledge of its futility. That is Camus's stark vision of the human condition. And yet he insists that we need to embrace it— that we must learn to treat "the struggle itself" as noble and thus as quite enough "to fill a man's heart." This leap of faith is perhaps the only way for an honest atheist to fulfill the haunting imperative with which Camus ends *The Myth of Sisyphus*: to "imagine Sisyphus happy."[35]

In several poignant and evocative poems, Philip Larkin explored a similar tension between atheism and happiness. From the wistful pointillism of "Church Going" (1955) to the mortal terror so startlingly expressed in "Aubade" (1977), Larkin made it clear that he thoroughly rejected faith in God and the afterlife. Yet these same poems also movingly and unforgettably describe the immense psychological struggles that often accompany atheism—an outlook he considered to be both "true" and "terrible." Religion—"That vast moth-eaten musical brocade / Created to pretend we never die"—used to dispel the terror of annihilation, or at least try to. But Larkin will have none of it, just as he dismisses the delusional equanimity before death that he finds in the writings of the ancient Epicureans. That leaves him—

and us—with no solace or reassurance, confronting the horrifying prospect of a lonely plunge into infinite nothingness:

> this is what we fear—no sight, no sound
> No touch or taste or smell, nothing to think with,
> Nothing to love or link with,
> The anesthetic from which none come round.[36]

But to reject religion does not merely entail facing our finitude without comforting illusions. It also involves the denial of something noble. It is perfectly fitting, Larkin seems to say, for an atheist to lament his lack of belief in a providential God who bestows metaphysical meaning on the full range of human desires and experiences. As he puts it in the unforgettable closing stanza of "Church Going," in which he ponders the prospect of a world without religion, the empty shell of the church he awkwardly inspects is a profoundly serious place; its seriousness flows from its capacity to serve as a location where our deepest spiritual needs and longings receive confirmation. In Larkin's view, the dignified beauty of religious ritual conceals the ugly truth under a layer of intricate artifice: the whole point of the liturgy performed on the church altar, Larkin implies, is to seduce us with the beautiful and supremely fulfilling illusion that our worldly compulsions have cosmological meaning and significance. For Larkin, this longing for our most precious hopes to link up with the order that governs the universe shows no signs of dying out; this aspect of religion, at least, may very well be too deeply rooted in the human soul ever to be completely purged.[37]

The compassionate generosity of Larkin's atheism reaches its peak in a third poem, "Faith Healing" from 1964. While the poem's first two stanzas rather cynically describe an American faith healer at a revival meeting devoting a few seconds of attention to each person's ailment

("*Now, dear child, / What's wrong*") before sending him away with a perfunctory prayer that elicits joyful tears, the third and final stanza strikes a very different tone. In the middle of the stanza's second line, Larkin abruptly halts his brutally mocking narrative in order to begin reflecting on the deepest sources of humanity's religious impulses. "In everyone there sleeps / A sense of life lived according to love," he proposes, and then immediately distinguishes between, first, those relative few who long to make a difference to others by loving them more fully and, second, the greater number who live lives of regret for "all they might have done had they been loved" by someone else.

Larkin suggests that human beings are creatures governed by love—by the longing to love and, even more so, by the longing to be loved. And in the curt sentence that follows these lines—"That nothing cures"—he indicates that this hunger can never be permanently satiated. But religion tries, understanding and responding to this crucially important aspect of humanity perhaps more fully than any other institution or practice. When the preacher looks into the eyes of the suffering parishioner, cradles her head in his hands, and utters "*Dear child*," Larkin writes, "an immense slackening ache / . . . Spreads slowly through" her, "As when, thawing, the rigid landscape weeps." The preacher's love may be a charade, the loving God that appears to act through him may be a fantasy conjured out of a combination of imagination and spiritual yearning, but in that moment faith has demonstrated its unique capacity to heal the human heart.[38]

Larkin was not alone in expressing profound ambivalence about his own atheism. Indeed, a rich tradition of modern thinking has denied God while also devoting itself to exploring the (usually negative) personal, moral, social, cultural, and even civilizational consequences of faithlessness. For Friedrich Nietzsche—the man who stands at the head of this tragic tradition—Socrates, Plato, and the rest of the Western philosophical tradition were delusional to assume that goodness, truth, and beauty imply or are even compatible with one another. "For a philosopher to say 'the good and the beautiful are one' is infamy; if he goes on to add, 'also the true,' one ought to thrash him. Truth is ugly."[39] Nearly everything Nietzsche wrote presupposed the ugliness of truth, with the ugliest truth of all being the complete absence of any overarching (moral or theological) order, meaning, or purpose to the universe.

This is a truth that will crush all but the very strongest men (such as Nietzsche himself), which means that the "death of God" in the modern West is a terrible problem, for individuals, for societies, for Western civilization, and even for the world as a whole, which is more deeply influenced by Western culture with every passing day.[40] As skepticism about a providential deity spreads throughout the world, the overwhelming majority of people will respond by becoming what Nietzsche called "last men"—namely, tame and timid hedonists utterly lacking in ambition or longing for greatness, including the distinctive greatness involved in attempting to live up to the exacting strictures imposed and demanded by biblical religion.[41] And therein lies Nietzsche's concern with the death of God: he feared it would lead to the abolition of man.[42]

Nietzsche believed that biblical religion was a lie, but also that it was a lie that contributed decisively to the flourishing of humanity—which is why he considered "unconditional honest atheism" to be an "awe-inspiring *catastrophe*." It was a catastrophe with only one conceivable solution: mankind would have to give itself, and then seek to live up to, a new life-giving lie. Much of Nietzsche's work can be seen as an attempt to wean his readers from the will to truth—the will that led modern man to "forbid itself the *lie involved in belief in God*" in the first place—in order to prepare them to accept just such a new lie.[43] But is it even conceivable that human beings would devote themselves to something that they understood to be untrue? Or would the authors of this new myth have to brainwash the rest of humanity into believing in its truth? And if so, would these authors eventually will themselves to forget the lie's dishonest origins through a form of self-imposed amnesia? Or, instead, would they have to settle for serving as humanity's propagandists, spreading salutary disinformation for the benefit of mankind, like puppetmasters in Plato's famous allegory projecting shadow images on the wall of the cave?

These are just some of the many puzzles generated by Nietzsche's catastrophic atheism—puzzles that would be taken up and developed in various ways by a wide range of twentieth-century playwrights, novelists, philosophers, and artists.[44] Though their anxious denial of God had little in common with the serene skepticism of their ancient counterparts, they shared with their classical forerunners—as well as with modern moralistic and stoic atheists—a keen sense of the social and existential complexities involved in denying the existence of providential gods.

5

In this sense, at least, all of these atheists were intellectually liberal, regardless of their (wildly differing and sometimes explicitly antiliberal) political views. Their liberalism consisted in their openness to complication and in their alertness to the tragic, irresolvable conflicts at the core of the human condition. They understood and accepted that although an individual may settle the question of God to his personal satisfaction, it is highly unlikely that all human beings will settle it in the same way—that differences in life experience, psychological makeup, social class, intelligence, the capacity for introspection, and temperament will tend to preclude unanimity about the fundamental mysteries of human existence, including God. A liberal atheist will tend to accept this situation; an ideological atheist will not.

That, in the end, is what separates the atheism of Socrates, Voltaire, and Larkin from the atheism of the French Revolution.

There can be little doubt about which group the new atheists belong to. Nearly everything they and their admirers say on the subject of religion is shot through with misanthropic enmity. Consider the case of P. Z. Myers, a biologist at the University of Minnesota–Morris, who writes a prominent Internet blog ("Pharyngula") on conflicts between science and religion. On July 8, 2008, he posted an item on his blog titled "It's a Frackin' Cracker" about a man named Webster Cook who had smuggled a consecrated host (or Eucharist)—a wafer that Roman Catholics believe to be the body of Christ—out of a Catholic Church.[45] For his prank, Cook was denounced by his local Catholic diocese and by Bill Donohue of the Catholic League for Religious and Civil Rights, an advocacy group, and he even received death threats.

In recounting this story, Myers was understandably outraged that devout Catholics had apparently threatened Cook. But Myers went much further than issuing a strongly worded criticism of such uncivilized behavior; he took the opportunity to describe Catholics who had been insulted by Cook's actions as "demented fuckwits" and dared his readers to steal consecrated Communion wafers from a local church and mail them to him so he could "joyfully and with laughter in my heart" desecrate these "goddamned cracker[s]" and then post the video of himself doing so on his website. Two weeks later, readers of Myers's blog had to settle for a photograph of a wafer in the trash, covered with coffee grounds and a banana peel, which is where he threw the "cracker" after piercing it with a rusty nail. The accompanying 2,300-word blog post (titled "The Great Desecration") reached its climax with the statement, "Nothing must be held sacred," printed in boldfaced type.[46]

It is P. Z. Myers's right, firmly rooted in American tradition and established in constitutional law, to engage in public acts of thuggish incivility. But that doesn't mean that his fellow citizens should respond passively to his vulgar display. On one level, it obviously doesn't matter very much that a handful of writers and entertainers have begun to reject liberal habits of mind and hatefully denounce the private beliefs of their fellow citizens. The United States remains a very religious nation. While there are small communities of atheists, agnostics, and skeptics in every state, and substantial ones in a few—Washington state leads the country with 25 percent of its residents claiming to worship no God; North Dakota comes in last with 3 percent—there aren't nearly enough unbelievers to leave a significant mark on the nation's culture or politics as a whole.[47]

Still, the rise of the new atheists is cause for concern—not among the targets of their anger, who can rest secure in the knowledge that the ranks of the religious will, here in America, dwarf the ranks of atheists for the foreseeable future, but rather among those for whom the defense of liberalism is a high priority. Of course, it is most likely liberals who propelled Dawkins, Harris, and Hitchens onto the bestseller lists by purchasing their books en masse—people who are worried about the dual threats to secular politics posed by militant Islam and the American religious right. These people are correct to be nervous about the future of liberalism, to perceive that it needs passionate, eloquent defenders. The problem is that the intellectual style of Dawkins, Harris, Hitchens, Maher, and Myers will undermine liberalism, not bolster it. Far from shoring up the secular political tradition, their arguments are likely to produce a country poised precariously between opposite and mutually antagonistic forms of illiberalism—as well as one in which traditionalist believers feel vindicated in their suspicion that a liberal society is fundamentally hostile to their convictions.

The last thing America needs is a war of attrition between two mutually exclusive, absolute systems of belief. Yet this is precisely what the new atheists appear to crave. The task for the rest of us—committed to neither dogmatic faith nor dogmatic disbelief—is to make certain that combatants on both sides of the theological divide fail to get their destructive way. What America needs now is not absolute faithlessness. It is intelligent faith and open-minded doubt.[48]

Epilogue

Religion in a Centerless Society

For the better part of the past 2,500 years, the political imagination of the Western world has been enchanted by an image of communal unity. The image emerged from the experience of life in the city-states of the ancient world, where philosophers suggested that a political community is a collective enterprise animated by a comprehensive vision of the highest human good, and that the content of this vision is determined by the individuals, families, factions, or classes that rule the community. Over the centuries, the image grew more elaborate. At some points, the community was described as a "ship of state" commanded by a brave and virtuous captain; at other times, it was a "body politic" whose head wisely guided the motions of its limbs. In every case, the image conveyed the view that politics is a contest over who will win the honor of standing at the *center* of a political community, serving as the *part* that fundamentally shapes its character as a *whole*.

This vision of politics was probably never anything more than a philosophical idealization covering over the complexities of ancient and medieval political life. Yet it captured something important about the character of politics in relatively homogeneous premodern societies—and especially about political life in Europe during the Middle Ages, when for several centuries the overarching institutional structure of the Catholic Church managed to contain many of the continent's social, cultural, and geographical tensions while also conferring a sense of shared metaphysical meaning on the hardships and suffering of daily life. In such a world, it was quite possible to imagine that each political community was a unified whole whose political and religious leaders were singularly dedicated to the spiritual betterment of the community's many parts.

Such edifying assumptions grew increasingly difficult to maintain in the wake of the Protestant Reformation, which irrevocably fractured European unity and transformed religion from a source of social harmony into a cause of rancorous division. Over the course of the sixteenth and seventeenth centuries, Europe broke apart into rival factions, each claiming to possess the absolute and universal truth in divine matters. The result was bloody civil wars of religion over radically conflicting and contradictory notions of the highest good.

For those who continued to think about politics in classical terms, the proper response to the religiously inspired violence unleashed by the Reformation was to use government power to restore lost communal unity and collective purpose. This approach was originally developed by champions of monarchical absolutism during the early modern period. It was later refined and radicalized by the totalitarian ideologies of the twentieth century. Today it lives on in Kim Jong-il's nightmarish North Korean tyranny and in the theocratic fantasies of al-Qaeda operatives and Taliban insurgents. But there was, and is, another option—the one devised and elaborated by theorists of political liberalism, who began their reflections by explicitly rejecting the image of politics that had dominated Western thinking since the time of the ancient Greeks.

Unlike so many of their predecessors and contemporaries, the first liberals treated disagreement and discord about the highest good as a given and then proposed that civil peace in a deeply divided society could best be established and maintained by excluding as much as possible the most divisive questions—metaphysical questions—from political life. Citizens would still have strongly held views about the highest good, but they would no longer presume that their neighbors or the political community as a whole would collectively endorse those views. Instead of articulating the community's shared vision of metaphysical truths, politics would focus on the more mundane task of securing the (economic and social) preconditions for individuals and groups to pursue the highest good, however they happened to define it.

Perhaps the most famous example of this liberal orientation can be found in the Declaration of Independence and its ringing invocation of a natural right of individuals to pursue happiness. The document's silence about the *content* of happiness and about what actions or ways of life are conducive to happiness would have been unthinkable in earlier forms of political thinking. But for a political liberal like Thomas Jefferson, the silence was an unavoidable outgrowth of the lack of a sufficient consensus regarding humanity's highest ends. Where such a consensus is lacking, it is foolish to expect more from politics—to expect the state to articulate and enforce a single, comprehensive notion of the highest good. Far from restoring the sense of spontaneous unity and shared meaning we like to see in pre-liberal forms of political life, such efforts would inevitably end up using state power to impose the values and beliefs of one part of a deeply divided community on its other parts.

Political liberalism was devised as a rescue operation for European life, mounted to meet a crisis set in motion by the rise of deep religious disagreement and the inability of earlier forms of political thought to make sense of it.[1] But liberalism doesn't just provide tools that make it possible for a society to manage pluralism. Once individuals and groups are granted the freedom to pursue the good as they wish, unburdened by the threat of political coercion, the political community becomes even more pluralistic than it already was—and in different ways than it already was. Visions of the highest good proliferate, setting individuals and groups off in different directions, pursuing happiness along divergent paths. In such a society, pluralism even seeps into individual lives, creating new, multifaceted forms of personal identity as well as a wide array of interwoven, rule-based social relationships.

Six days a week my mailman delivers mail to my home—not because of his benevolence or public-spiritedness, but because he abides by the rules of his job. But at the same time, those rules do not fundamentally define him; the task of delivering the mail is merely a part of his life—merely one aspect of his identity. He may also be a devoted husband and father of two young children, a lapsed Catholic, an avid football fan, a member of the town council, an occasional bowler, a staunch Republican, an ex-Deadhead, a regular and enthusiastic viewer of *Top Chef*, a proud third-generation Italian American, and so forth, through all of the disparate goods he pursues in the multiple aspects of his private and public lives. Each of these aspects and each of these pursuits tell us *something* about his identity, but none of them should be confused with its essence, with its core, with *who he is as a whole*, which is somehow the totality of these various aspects and pursuits, and their complicated interrelations—just as a liberal society is somehow the totality of the various pursuits of every individual within it.

These are some of the overlapping centrifugal tendencies of modern liberalism—of a society devoted to individual freedom, of a political community in which questions concerning the highest good have been displaced from a position of public primacy. It is, in a word, a *centerless society*—and one that grows ever more centerless, more differentiated, more pluralistic over time.[2] This is not to say that all liberal societies are equally centerless. In Europe, where the liberal idea was born, cultural and ethnic homogeneity have acted as a brake on the process of social differentiation, as they have to an even greater extent in Japan and other Asian nations. It is in the United States, with its large population, vast size, highly dynamic capitalist economy, and ethnically heterogeneous population united by little besides the liberal creed classically expressed in the Declaration of Independence, that centerlessness has been taken to its greatest extreme, creating a society with no single center and no part that can claim unchallenged supremacy over the country as a whole.

Nowhere is American centerlessness more apparent than in religion. In the nearly four centuries since the first dissenting Protestants arrived in New England seeking the freedom to worship, religion has proliferated far beyond anyone's conceivable prediction. Thanks in large part to the liberal bargain at the heart of the First Amendment—which requires religious groups to give up their desire to seek the establishment of a particular religion in return for the virtually unlimited free exercise of faith—the Protestant churches brought to American shores from the Old World have splintered countless times, giving birth to multitudes of new sects, and even entirely new religions.[3] But the story of religion in the United States is hardly limited to Protestantism, or even to Christianity. Roman Catholicism has taken root and flourished, becoming in the course of the twentieth century the single largest Christian denomination in the country, while Judaism has thrived to such an extent that the Jewish experience in America has raised questions

for the Zionist project, showing at long last that it is possible for
Jews to live and prosper in peace and safety in a majority-Christian
nation. Then there are Unitarianism, Eastern Orthodoxy, Islam,
Buddhism, Hinduism, sundry New Age faiths, and thousands of
smaller groups, each of them worshipping, praying, and preaching
in their own ways, with each of their members free to dissent and
set out on a new spiritual path, which they often do.

It is an enormous human achievement—allowing people to seek
and find religious meaning in their lives without fear of government
coercion, and in the process creating a centerless society of mind-
boggling diversity and complexity. Yet religion is also where the centerless society encounters its greatest, and gravest, test. The trouble
comes from specifically traditionalist religion and its belief in comprehensive spiritual and moral truths—truths that sometimes clash
with the preconditions of liberal politics and social centerlessness.
When the urge to seek purity through social and political withdrawal
becomes more than a personal quest and starts to be treated as a
preliminary step toward cleansing the nation as a whole of spiritual
contaminants, it raises the specter of theologically inspired conflict
and oppression. When authoritarian elements of religion seep into
the political world, believers find themselves torn between theological and political loyalties. When the faithful denounce the pursuit of
knowledge about the world, they produce a population incapable of
acting as thoughtful and informed citizens. When religious groups
view the nation's politics and history through the lens of divine providence, they promise a false clarity that simplifies and distorts our
understanding of the country's actions in the world. When traditionalists attempt to use the law to impose their vision of sexual morality
on the nation as a whole, they show that they have failed to com-
prehend the ineradicably pluralistic character of a centerless society.
Even the rejection of God, when it becomes a counter-religion with

its own absolute moral imperatives, can test the liberal order by fostering social intolerance, promoting the idea of coercive secularization, and inflaming fears among already paranoid elements of the religious right.

Non-liberal governments frequently outlaw groups that fundamentally challenge them. But liberalism is committed to upholding religious freedom. That commitment has given rise to an alternative view, elegantly captured in the famous metaphor of a wall of separation between church and state. In the separationist ideal, religion is completely cordoned off from politics but left free to thrive in the private sphere of people's lives. It is a noble vision—one that powerfully expresses the core liberal conviction that religion and politics both benefit from keeping out of each other's business. But the metaphor is also deceptive, implying as it does that it's possible to construct a settled, fixed, permanent, impenetrable legal barrier between the parties.

A better image might be an endlessly shifting skirmish line, with each party constantly pushing back against the incursions of the other, adjusting its arguments and tactics as circumstances and situations change over time. On one side, each religious group attempts to take and hold territory it views as vital to its survival and its theologically inspired vision of the world. (Sometimes the religious groups even band together to fight for a common cause, as traditionalist Protestants, Catholics, Mormons, and other churches have repeatedly done over the mainly sexual issues at the heart of the post-1960s culture war.) Meanwhile, on the other side of the line, the liberal state seeks to balance the freedom of innumerable competing individuals and groups against each other as well as against the common good of the centerless society as a whole. Unlike a wall, which once built can only be either defended or torn down, a skirmish line is dynamic, changing its shape, size, and location as a direct result of variations in hostility between the competing parties and in direct response to the relative strength of the argumentative firepower deployed by each side. That, it appears, is our fate—and the liberal promise: to fight out our theological–political differences without end, one battle at a time, using reasons instead of rifles.

The conflict between politics and religion will not end anytime soon, or ever. But the intensity of the clash might be diminished by reflection on the more or less permanent tensions between devout belief and the liberal order.[4] History shows us that traditionalist religion and various forms of non-liberal government (theocracy, absolute monarchy) can be compatible. The same can be said of strident atheism and totalitarianism. Conversely, when religion is liberal—when it makes few supernatural claims, when it is doctrinally minimal, and when it serves primarily as a repository of moral wisdom—it can play a significant public role in a liberal society. This is what America's constitutional framers—most of them liberal Christians or deists who believed that God plays little to no providential role in the world—meant when they spoke about religion contributing to the stability and flourishing of the nation's liberal system of government. In our own time, sociologist Christian Smith has argued that many American teenagers and young adults espouse similarly lukewarm religious views, which he dubs Moralistic Therapeutic Deism.[5] Whether such beliefs are politically beneficial or merely innocuous, they pose no serious challenge to the liberal order of the United States.

The relationship between traditionalist religion and liberal politics is far more contentious. In a liberal political community, devout believers will be free within very broad limits to live their faith, and in most cases they will be quite capable of fulfilling the (relatively limited) ordinary duties of citizenship: voting, paying taxes, occasionally sitting on juries, serving in the armed forces when called to defend the nation in times of war. Yet even in these seemingly easy cases, there will sometimes be difficulties for the most intensely religious. The Amish in the United States refuse to serve in the military, for example, as do Haredi Jews in Israel. Likewise, the ritual observances of many faiths may at times make it difficult for their members to vote or fulfill jury duty.

Tensions increase exponentially as we approach the most intense forms of piety and the most exalted forms of citizenship (which involve serving in high political office). A deeply devout believer—someone who places his faith at the center of his life—will tend to think of himself first and foremost as a member of the one true church working toward the establishment of the kingdom of God under Jesus Christ, if not in this life, then in the next. His ultimate loyalty will be to Christ, just as the ultimate loyalty of the most observant Jew will be to God and the Torah, while a Muslim's will be to Allah and the Koran. Liberal citizenship at its peak, by contrast, requires devotion to the liberal institutions and democratically enacted laws of the political community above all else. That's why American presidents and other high officials swear an oath to uphold the Constitution of the United States and not natural or divine law of any kind.

These divergent loyalties might not come into direct conflict every day, but they nonetheless stand in deep and abiding tension with one another, forever threatening to pit the theological duties of the devout believer against the political duties of the citizen. The tension increases the closer we come to the peak of political power. A devout Mormon can serve as the mayor of Provo, Utah, without failing the religious test, for example, both because the population of Provo is 88 percent Mormon and because the political power wielded by mayors is checked by numerous higher-ranking officials, including the state governor and legislature as well as several state and federal courts. The same dynamic applies, in reverse, to a doctrinally committed atheist running for mayor of San Francisco, Seattle, or another similarly secular urban area. A devout Mormon or proselytizing atheist running for president of the United States, however, is a very different and far more troubling prospect.

It is possible for someone of liberal or moderate belief to be a great president—because his faith will make few potentially uncompromising, illiberal demands on him. The same cannot be said of the most devout believers, who face a stark choice. Either they can practice the art of drawing distinctions between their piety and the nation's politics, or they can refrain from seeking high political office. What will never be possible is a theological–political synthesis. As long as the United States remains a liberal nation with a centerless society, traditionalist religion at its peak will fail to harmonize with politics at its peak. Our saints will not be statesmen and our statesmen will not be saints. That is perhaps the most important and enduring lesson to be learned from the religious test.

Acknowledgments

The great literary critic Lionel Trilling once famously described his life's work as taking place at the "dark and bloody crossroads where literature and politics meet." Trilling wasn't normally given to hyperbole. Yet I wonder: if the intersection between literature and politics is dark and bloody, how to describe the place where religion and politics converge? A corpse-strewn battlefield? A pestilential swamp? The metaphorical possibilities are endless, if a little overwrought. Let's just say that writing critically about religion and politics isn't the most efficient way to make friends and influence people. And that makes me all the more grateful for those who have supported the work that went into researching and writing this book.

For the past several years the Center for Programs in Contemporary Writing at the University of Pennsylvania has provided an exciting environment in which to teach and write. I am especially grateful to Valerie Ross, the intellectual and administrative dynamo behind Penn's Critical Writing Program, for her friendship and professional support. Thanks also to the Department of Religious Studies at Penn—in particular to E. Ann Matter, Talya Fishman, and Annette Y. Reed—for inviting me to teach courses in the department and participate in its weekly colloquia.

The idea for the book grew out of a long, invigorating lunch with Tina Bennett. Mark Lilla and Alan Wolfe provided encouragement and valuable advice at early stages of the project. Chapters Two and Six began as articles in the *New Republic*, while numerous other passages in the book first appeared on my blog at the magazine's website. I'd like to offer special thanks to *TNR* editors Frank Foer, Richard Just, Greg Veis, and Leon Wieseltier for giving me the opportunity to contribute to a magazine that does so much to uphold the ideal of exacting intellectuality that Trilling and the other New York critics once exemplified and that I strive in my own modest way to match.

I presented an early version of my critique of American providentialism at a conference on "The Future of Political Theologies" at Georgetown University's Berkley Center for Religion, Peace, and World Affairs. I'd like to thank Michael Kessler for the invitation to participate and several of the other participants (including Jerome Copulsky, Eric Gregory, Charles Mathewes, and Erik Owens) for their valuable comments and criticisms.

My arguments were revised and refined through often intense intellectual discussion, and sometimes combat, with a number of friends and acquaintances: Peter Agree, J. Scott Craig, Rebecca Davis, Ross Douthat, Rod Dreher, Bryan Earl, Russell Arben Fox, Sarah Hammond, Ed Kilgore, Noah Millman, William Ruger, Matthew Stannard, Andrew Sullivan, and Matthew Yglesias. At Norton, Alane Salierno Mason has been an ideal editor, providing timely and tough-minded feedback that substantially improved every chapter as well as the shape of the book as a whole.

And then there are my debts to my family, which belong in a

separate category. My wife, Beth Linker, is my touchstone, sounding board, critical eye, and partner in everything, from parenting to brainstorming for blog posts. Some days I don't know how we keep our indescribably hectic household from flying apart in a million directions. But somehow we manage to make it work, binding it together with bonds of time-tested love and devotion. There's no one with whom I'd rather be sharing the adventure.

To my children Mark and Kaitlyn, to whom this book is dedicated, I am grateful beyond words—above all, for the gift of perspective. We toil, we strive, we play, we think, we laugh, we love, we endure—we live—whether or not we have children. But nothing in life teaches clarity and humility like the incomparable experience of holding your suffering child in your arms while you offer everything you have, and it amounts only to impotent consolation. What is the worth of politics at such moments? Not very much, I'm afraid. But still there are tasks to be done, books to be written—though now with lucidity. That is the gift. And these paltry pages are mine, offered humbly in return.

Notes

I The Imperative of Religious Freedom

1 Statistics in Donald B. Kraybill, *The Riddle of Amish Culture*, revised edition (Baltimore: Johns Hopkins University Press, 2001), 335–36. Two-thirds of the Amish can be found in Pennsylvania, Ohio, and Indiana.

2 See Richard A. Stevick, *Growing Up Amish: The Teenage Years* (Baltimore: Johns Hopkins University Press, 2007), 6; and Kraybill, *The Riddle of Amish Culture*, 7.

3 The Mennonites broke from the Amish in 1693 over the practice of shunning excommunicated members of the community, with the former taking a more liberal view. To this day, the Mennonites place somewhat fewer barriers between themselves and the modern world. Hutterites, by contrast, are a bit more radical than the Amish, adding a form of communal ownership to the long list of practices that separate them from the rest of modern America.

4 Kraybill, *The Riddle of Amish Culture*, 13.

5 Kraybill, "Negotiating with Caesar," in Donald B. Kraybill, ed., *The Amish and the State* (Baltimore: Johns Hopkins University Press, 1993), 9, 12–13.

6 See Stevick, *Growing Up Amish*, 61.

7 Ibid., 72, 62.

8 Ibid., 22.

9 This would explain why the more conservative Old Order churches have much higher rates of retention than more progressive New Order ones. See ibid., 235.

10 Kraybill, "Negotiating with Caesar," 16, 8–9.

11 Ibid., 9–10. Stevick, *Growing Up Amish*, 237.

12 Kraybill, "Negotiating with Caesar," 17. The social harmony enjoyed by the Amish also helps to explain why they tend not to employ the forms of alternative dispute resolution favored by Haredi Jews and traditionalist Muslims. See the discussion below.

13 Ibid., 17–18.

14 Through farming, small business enterprises, and tourism, the Amish are actually quite integrated into the broader economic life of their regions.

15 See the discussion in Samuel Heilman, *Defenders of the Faith: Inside Ultra-Orthodox Jewry* (Berkeley: University of California Press, 2000), 18.

16 Ibid., 21–24.

17 Ibid., 25, 35.

18 Ibid., 12.

19 Karelitz quoted in ibid., 38.

20 Samuel Heilman, *Sliding to the Right: The Contest for the Future of American Jewish Orthodoxy* (Berkeley: University of California Press, 2006), 28–30.

21 Ibid., 2, 7, 63–65, 75.

22 See ibid., 27, 81–82, 300–301. See also the quote on 58–59 from Rabbi Herschel Schachter, a prominent student of Rabbi Joseph Soloveitchik, the founder of modern Orthodoxy: God "forbids us to display any interest in any other religion. We are not permitted to attend a religious service of any other faith, or even watch it on television. We may not study works of or about any other religion, watch films about them, or study any piece of religious art. A Jew may not enter a house of worship of any other religion even during the hours that services are not being held. We may not even 'utter upon our lips' the name of any other god." That a prominent student of the founder of modern Orthodoxy now makes such separatist declarations is a vivid sign of its drift in the direction of Haredism. For more on these trends, see Alan Mittleman, "Fretful Orthodoxy," *First Things*, October 2003.

23 Heilman, *Sliding to the Right*, 64–65, 75. Interestingly, Domino's Pizza founder Thomas Monaghan appears to be following the separatist model of the Haredim in his efforts to build a homogeneously orthodox Catholic university and town (both called Ave Maria) in the swamplands east of Naples, Florida. For more on Monaghan's efforts, see Damon Linker, *The Theocons* (New York: Doubleday, 2006), 195–96.

24 For more on the role of suburbanization in American Jewish life, see Jonathan D. Sarna, *American Judaism: A History* (New Haven, CT, and London: Yale University Press, 2004), 282ff.

25 Heilman, *Sliding to the Right*, 327–28, n. 20.

26 Ibid., 81–82, 300–301.

27 American policy toward the state of Israel plays less of a role in determining the voting patterns of the Haredi community in the United States than one might expect. Most Haredim reject the secular ideology of Zionism, maintaining that the true political independence of the Jewish people can only be realized by the Messiah; and that inspires deeply rooted ambivalence about Israel and its fate. This hasn't stopped hundreds of thousands of Haredi Jews from making their home in the state of Israel, however.

28 The situation in Israel, where Haredi Jews make up 15–20 percent of the population and thus wield significant political power through the country's system of proportional representation, is far less benign. Not only are the Haredim granted a religiously based exclusion from service in the Israeli army, which greatly heightens their alienation from their fellow citizens, all the rest of whom are required to serve, but the Israeli government subsidizes Haredi yeshiva study, which enables them to withdraw almost completely from the modern life of the nation into purely religious concerns and fixations. The practical effect of these policies is to serve as a government-sponsored program fostering a radically right-wing sectarian movement within Israeli society, the consequences of which over the long term are unlikely to be good.

29 See Eugene Volokh, "Sharia Law Enforced in Texas!" *The Volokh Conspiracy*, February 8, 2008, http://www.volokh.com/posts/1202454061.shtml.

30 "Faith, Law, and Democracy: Defining the Limits of Exceptionalism," *Economist*, February 14, 2008. See also "Islam and the Law," *Economist*, February 9, 2008. For a particularly vitriolic response to Williams's proposal, see Christopher Hitchens, "To Hell with the Archbishop of Canterbury," *Slate*, February 11, 2008.

31 "Faith, Law, and Democracy: Defining the Limits of Exceptionalism," *Economist*, February 14, 2008.

32 Among its many views, this ideology holds that fundamentalist readings of the Koran are the only valid ones, that the world is divided between Muslims and their enemies, that Jews and Christians deliberately act to destroy Muslims, and that Muslims must control political power in order to thrive.

33 Paul M. Barrett, *American Islam: The Struggle for the Soul of a Religion* (New York: Farrar, Straus and Giroux, 2007), 10–11.

34 For deeply troubling data on widespread abuse within the Muslim community of Great Britain, see "Crimes of the Community: Honour-Based Violence in the UK," a report published by the Center for Social Cohesion, a London-based think tank, www.socialcohesion.co.uk/pdf/CrimesOfTheCommunity.pdf.

35   See "Muslims in Europe: Country Guide," BBC News, December 23, 2005, http://news.bbc.co.uk/2/hi/europe/4385768.stm#uk.

36   Barrett, *American Islam*, 10. For an enlightening study of France's difficulties with integrating its large community of Algerian, Moroccan, and Tunisian Muslims, see Jonathan Laurence and Justin Vaisse, *Integrating Islam: Political and Religious Challenges in Contemporary France* (Washington, DC: Brookings Institution Press, 2006). For a more polemical study of Muslims in Europe, see Christopher Caldwell, *Reflections on the Revolution in Europe: Immigration, Islam, and the West* (New York: Doubleday, 2009).

37   Barrett, *American Islam*, 6–7, 8–9. In college, observant Muslims tend to gravitate toward fields, such as engineering and the applied sciences, that do not conflict with their faith.

38   Ibid., 5.

39   For one discouraging sign that this has indeed been the effect of political and cultural developments over the past decade, see Neil MacFarquhar's *New York Times* article about a dramatic spike in home-schooling by families of South Asian Muslim girls in Lodi, California: "Resolute or Fearful, Many Muslims Turn to Home Schooling," *New York Times*, March 26, 2008.

40   Such rhetoric permeated the GOP primary campaigns of 2007–2008.

41   No one knows precisely how tiny. Leaders of the movement have claimed as many as 20 million followers, though most informed observers estimate their numbers to be much smaller, perhaps in the tens of thousands.

42   Michelle Goldberg, *Kingdom Coming: The Rise of Christian Nationalism* (New York: W. W. Norton, 2006), and Kevin Phillips, *American Theocracy: The Peril and Politics of Radical Religion, Oil, and Borrowed Money in the 21st Century* (New York: Viking, 2006).

43   Quoted in John R. Pottenger, *Reaping the Whirlwind: Liberal Democracy and the Religious Axis* (Washington DC: Georgetown University Press, 2007), 212–13. As Pottenger goes on to point out, the NRA continues to call for an amendment to modify the Preamble to the Constitution.

44   Ibid., 217, 218–19, 221.

45   Rushdoony quoted in ibid., 224–25.

46   Goldberg, *Kingdom Coming*, 41.

47   For PCA statistics, see http://www.pcaac.org/statistics.htm.

48   North quoted in Goldberg, *Kingdom Coming*, 14.

49   DeMar quoted in Pottenger, *Reaping the Whirlwind*, 227–28.

50   Kennedy quoted in ibid., 235–36. Pottenger lists several other organizations as contributing to this mission, including the Ohio Restoration Project, Alliance Defense Fund, American Family Association, American Vision, Chalcedon

Foundation, Council for National Policy, Family Research Council, Institute for Christian Economics, Rutherford Institute, and WallBuilders.

51   See Mitchell L. Stevens, *Kingdom of Children: Culture and Controversy in the Homeschooling Movement* (Princeton, NJ: Princeton University Press, 2001), 5, 24–25, 34ff.

52   Ibid., 26–27, 40.

53   "The Condition of Education 2009," National Center for Education Statistics, 2009-081, U.S. Department of Education: http://nces.ed.gov/programs/coe/2009/pdf/6_2009.pdf.

54   Hanna Rosin, *God's Harvard: A Christian College on a Mission to Save America* (Orlando: Harcourt, Inc., 2007), 62.

55   Stevens, *Kingdom of Children*, 14.

56   Rosin, *God's Harvard*, 62.

57   Michael Farris quoted in ibid., 62.

58   These statistics are often compiled using unscientific methods, like self-reporting of results, and used to bolster the position of the home-schooling movement. For example, see the impressive-sounding statistics compiled by the HSLDA: http://www.hslda.org/docs/nche/000010/200410250.asp.

59   See Stevens, *Kingdom of Children*, 54–55, and Rosin, *God's Harvard*, 114ff. Besides A Beka Book, Christian home-schoolers can choose from a selection of textbooks by such publishers as Providence Press, Alpha Omega Publications, KONOS, Bob Jones University Press, Christian Liberty Academy, the Weaver Curriculum Series, Advanced Training Institute International, and several others.

60   As Stevens notes (*Kingdom of Children*, 11), 98 percent of home-schoolers are white.

61   For use of the language of "dirt" and "contagion" among Christian home-schoolers, see ibid., 51–53.

62   Farris quoted in Rosin, *God's Harvard*, 45.

63   Ibid., 17, 13.

64   Ibid., 21, where Farris is quoted as saying, "I don't care what Plato says. We don't need the world's knowledge and information to *guide* us. This is basically what's called opposition research." See also 262, where Farris declares, "I've read seventy pages of the *Iliad* this weekend and it's rubbish; it's all about adultery. I can write better than that."

65   Ibid., 258–62.

66   Ibid., 47–48: "Nearly every conservative Republican senator or congressman has had a Patrick Henry student work on his or her staff or campaign."

67   Aside from the matter of principle, liberals have strong prudential reasons to avoid picking a fight with home-schoolers by seeking to reverse the right to

educate children at home. Once a right has been granted, it cannot be taken away without generating publicity and sympathy for those on the losing end. And the state should do everything it can to avoid turning the Michael Farrises of the nation into victims or martyrs.

68 See, for example, the educational films produced by an organization called Youth in Motion (http://frameline.org/youthinmotion/index.html), which provides "free LGBT themed movies to student clubs and teachers in middle and high schools throughout California" and describes its goal as giving "student activists and teachers new tools to educate their peers about lesbian, gay, bisexual, and transgender history and culture (and have fun doing it!)." The group claims that more than 250 schools in California have registered to receive its materials. How many teachers have actually shown these films to students is anyone's guess.

69 For more on this topic, see the discussion in the following chapter.

II The Dangers of Divine Authority

1 The conflict had roots deep in the American past. Roman Catholics were a small minority in the early colonies (the first diocese, in Baltimore, was established only in 1789), and they were immersed in a spiritual culture very different than the ones that prevailed in the more religiously homogeneous nations of Europe. Whereas the church was accustomed to ordering itself as a strict hierarchy with clear lines of authority and rules of obedience, the form of ecclesiastical organization that prevailed in the early American colonies was the congregationalism of New England Puritanism, in which members of a parish shared ownership of church property as well as the responsibility for hiring and firing pastors and other church officials. For a time, from 1815 to 1830, Catholics in New York, Philadelphia, Charleston, SC, and other cities sought to Americanize the church in the United States, instituting a unique form of congregational Catholicism in which churches would be owned and run by lay Catholic boards of trustees. This so-called trusteeism controversy pitted most bishops and the entire Vatican hierarchy against some priests and large numbers of American Catholic laypeople over the issue of whether Catholicism in America would be restructured along egalitarian lines. In the end, Rome prevailed in the dispute and trusteeism was suppressed, with the American church adopting the same hierarchical structure that prevails in other nations. What happened in Connecticut during the first two weeks of March 2009 was thus a brief revival of the trusteeism controversy in our own time. The revival was led by a Catholic group, Voice of the Faithful (VOTF),

that had been formed in response to the sexual abuse scandals that roiled the church in 2002 and 2003. Inspired by the writings of prominent liberal Catholic academics such as Paul Lakeland and David O'Brien and provoked by ongoing incidences of alleged parish misgovernance in Connecticut—including a 2006 fraud case in which Michael Jude Fay, a priest of the diocese of Bridgeport, was accused of embezzling $1.4 million from his parish—VOTF began lobbying for lay control of the church within the state. For a few days, it looked like the group might succeed in its efforts, but a furious outcry from Catholics in Connecticut, not to mention a statement of protest from the US Conference of Catholic Bishops in Washington, DC, led the bill to be abandoned very quickly.

2   Kenneth D. Wald, Dennis E. Owen, and Samuel S. Hill, Jr., "Habits of the Mind? The Problem of Authority in the New Christian Right," in Ted G. Jelen, ed., *Religion and Political Behavior in the United States* (New York: Praeger, 1989), 95–96.

3   See Nancy Tatom Ammerman, *Bible Believers: Fundamentalism in the Modern World* (Piscataway, NJ: Rutgers University Press, 1987), 128: "[Believers] come to expect groups to be divided between sheep and shepherds. The shepherds are entitled to deference and rewards, while the sheep are entitled to love and care." See also Brenda E. Brasher, *Godly Women: Fundamentalism and Female Power* (Piscataway, NJ: Rutgers University Press, 1998). It is most likely the love, care, and protection owed to subordinates that explains the "warm, expressive" style of parenting that W. Bradford Wilcox finds among evangelicals. See Wilcox, "Conservative Protestant Childrearing: Authoritarian or Authoritative?" *American Sociological Review* 63, no. 6 (December 1998), 796–809.

4   John P. Bartkowski and Christopher G. Ellison, "Divergent Models of Child rearing in Popular Manuals: Conservative Protestants vs. the Mainstream Experts," *Sociology of Religion* 56, no. 1 (Spring 1995), 25–27.

5   Ibid., 29.

6   Christopher G. Ellison, John P. Bartkowski, and Michelle L. Segal, "Do Conservative Protestant Parents Spank More Often? Further Evidence from the National Survey of Families and Households," *Social Science Quarterly* 77, no. 3 (September 1996), 663–73.

7   Christopher G. Ellison and Darren E. Sherkat, "Conservative Protestantism and Support for Capital Punishment," *American Sociological Review* 58, no. 1 (February 1993), 131–44. As of spring 2009, less than half of the general public (49 percent) said that government-sponsored torture could "often" or "sometimes" be justified, compared with almost two-thirds of white evangelicals (62 percent). See the Pew Forum for Religion and Public Life, April 29,

2009, updated May 7, 2009: "The Religious Dimensions of the Torture Debate," http://pewforum.org/docs/?DocID=156.

8 See "A Look at Religious Voters in the 2008 Election," Pew Research Center Publications, February 10, 2009, http://pewresearch.org/pubs/1112/religion-vote-2008-election.

9 See, for instance, Ronald Smothers, "The 1992 Campaign: Conservatives; Bush Gets Two Cheers from Religious Right," *New York Times*, March 10, 1992. In the end, evangelicals gave 56 percent of their votes to Bush in the three-way race against Bill Clinton and Ross Perot.

10 Clinton received less than a quarter of the white evangelical vote in 1992 and just 31 percent in 1996. See Robert Booth Fowler, Allen D. Hertzke, and Laura R. Olson, *Religion and Politics in America: Faith, Culture, and Strategic Choices* (Boulder, CO: Westview Press, 1999), 101–2.

11 According to the National Election Study of 1998, 56 percent of "committed evangelical Protestants" favored impeachment of Clinton over the Lewinsky scandal, the highest level of any religious subgroup included in the survey. See Andrew Kohut, John C. Green, Scott Keeter, and Robert C. Toth, *The Diminishing Divide: Religion's Changing Role in American Politics* (Washington, DC: Brookings Institution Press, 2000), 93.

12 See Joel Rosenberg, "Flash Traffic: Political Buzz from Washington," *World*, October 6, 2001, at http://www.worldmag.com/display-article.cfm?id=5425. See also David Kirkpatrick, "Aide Is Bush's Eyes and Ears on the Right," *New York Times*, June 28, 2004.

13 "Religion and the Presidential Vote: Bush's Gains Broad-Based," Pew Research Center for the People and the Press, December 6, 2004, http://people-press.org/commentary/?analysisid=103.

14 For example, in June 2007 Bush's job approval among white evangelicals over thirty was 52 percent, while it was 45 percent for those between the ages of eighteen and twenty-nine. By contrast, the comparable numbers for Americans as a whole were 33 percent and 28 percent. See "Young White Evangelicals: Less Republican, Still Conservative," Pew Research Center Publications, September 28, 2007, http://pewresearch.org/pubs/605/young-white-evangelicals-less-republican-still-conservative.

15 Jay Newton-Small, "Interview with Sarah Palin," *Time*, August 29, 2008.

16 Claire Suddath, "Conservative Believer," *Time*, August 29, 2008, http://www.time.com/time/specials/packages/article/0,28804,1837523_1837531_1837538,00.html.

17 Jon Cohen and Jennifer Agiesta, "Perceptions of Palin Grow Increasingly Negative, Poll Says," *Washington Post*, October 25, 2008.

18 For more on the role of sincerity in shaping evangelical political judgment, see Alan Wolfe, "A God That Never Failed," *New Republic*, November 6, 2006.

19 Pew Research Center Publications, "Voting Religiously," November 5, 2008, http://pewresearch.org/pubs/1022/exit-poll-analysis-religion. Bush won 50.7 percent of the popular vote in 2004, while Obama won 52.9 percent in 2008—meaning that in both elections the Catholic vote approximated the final result to within 1.5 percentage points.

20 To be precise, whereas 53 percent of Americans believe abortion should be legal in all or most cases, the number is 48 percent among Catholics. The same five-point gap is present when the question is whether abortion should be illegal in all or most cases: 40 percent for the US population as a whole versus 45 percent for Catholics. See The Pew Forum on Religion and Public Life, "Abortion Views by Religious Affiliation," January 15, 2009, http://pewforum.org/docs/?DocID=384.

21 Harris Poll #78, October 20, 2005, http://www.harrisinteractive.com/harris_poll/index.asp?PID=608.

22 John Henry Newman, *Apologia Pro Vita Sua* (London: Fontana Books, 1959; originally published 1864), 276.

23 John T. McGreevy, *Catholicism and American Freedom: A History* (New York: W. W. Norton, 2003), 36–7.

24 Theodore Parker quoted in ibid., 34.

25 See Timothy M. Dolan, "The Bishops in Council," *First Things*, April 2005, 20–21. Dolan is currently serving as the Archbishop of New York.

26 For more on the Americanist heresy, see Thomas T. McAvoy, *The Americanist Heresy in Roman Catholicism* (Notre Dame, IN: Notre Dame Press, 1963), and the useful Internet article by Aaron Massey, "The Phantom Heresy?": http://are.as.wvu.edu/massey.htm.

27 Dolan, "The Bishops in Council," 23.

28 See, for example, John Courtney Murray, *We Hold These Truths: Catholic Reflections on the American Proposition* (Lanham, MD: Rowman & Littlefield, 1960).

29 See *Dignitatis Humanae*, Par. 9. Promulgated by His Holiness Pope Paul VI on December 7, 1965. Murray's position on these issues was so controversial when he first published them, in a series of academic articles in the early 1950s, that his superiors forbade him to continue writing on the topic.

30 For a relatively recent example of the attempt to Catholicize liberalism, see Richard John Neuhaus, "The Liberalism of John Paul II," *First Things*, May 1997.

31 For more on the intra-Catholic debate about how the church should respond to pro-choice Catholics, see Damon Linker, *Theocons*, 168–75.

32 This argument was frequently made by the late Father Richard John Neuhaus

and his conservative allies in the bishops' conference. See, for example, "Communion & *Communio*," The Public Square, *First Things*, August/September 2004, 86–89.

33 Much of this unusual theological position was revealed by Joseph Smith in a speech in April 1844 called the "King Follitt Discourse," http://mldb.byu.edu/follett.htm.

34 For more on historic end points for Christian prophecy, see Niels Christian Hvidt, *Christian Prophecy: The Post-Biblical Tradition* (New York: Oxford University Press, 2007), 3–21.

35 See Hobbes, *Leviathan* (Cambridge, MA: Hackett, 1994; originally published 1660), 3.7; 7.7; 8.25; 32.7, 9; 34.13; 36.9–10, 19–20; 37.13.

36 Bruce R. McConkie, *Personal Testimony of Personal Revelation on Priesthood* (Salt Lake City: Deseret Book Company, 1981), 126–37. See also James E. Talmage, *Articles of Faith* (Salt Lake City: Deseret Book Company, 1984), 275–76: "Revelation is essential to the Church, not only for the proper calling and ordination of its ministers but also that the officers so chosen may be guided in their administrations—to teach with authority the doctrines of salvation, to admonish, to encourage, and if necessary to reprove the people, and to declare unto them by prophecy the purposes and will of God respecting the Church, present and future."

37 The document can be found online at http://www.lds-mormon.com/fourteen.shtml.

38 Emphases added.

39 Richard Lyman Bushman, *Joseph Smith: Rough Stone Rolling* (New York: Knopf, 2005), 129.

40 Ibid., 172.

41 Richard Bushman attempted to make this case in an online debate with me at the *New Republic*: http://www.tnr.com/article/politics/mitt-romneys-mormonism.

42 Bushman, *Joseph Smith*, 175.

43 Ibid., 257–58.

44 Ibid., 257.

45 Ibid., 175.

46 See the American Association of University Professors report, "Academic Freedom and Tenure: Brigham Young University," *Academe*, September–October 1997.

47 Joseph Fielding Smith, *Doctrines of Salvation*, 3 vols. (Salt Lake City: Bookcraft, 1954), 3:203.

48 Quoted in Ezra Taft Benson, "Fourteen Fundamentals in Following the Prophet," February 26, 1980, http://www.lds-mormon.com/fourteen.shtml.

49 Heber C. Kimball (first counselor to Young in the First Presidency) quoted in Richard Abanes, *One Nation Under Gods: A History of the Mormon Church* (New York: Four Walls Eight Windows, 2002), 221–23.

50 Brigham Young quoted in ibid., 221. See also p. 219, where Abanes writes: "The kingdom of God on earth that Brigham envisioned was vast. So after arriving in the Salt Lake area, he laid claim to all lands stretching west to east from San Diego to the crest of the Rocky Mountains (near present-day Denver), and north to south from the Wind River Mountains of Wyoming to Arizona's Gila River. Zion, as originally staked out by Young . . . totaled about 265,000 square miles, or roughly one-sixth of America's current geography."

51 See Jon Krakauer, *Under the Banner of Heaven: A Story of Violent Faith* (New York: Doubleday, 2003). It is unclear whether Mormon Russell Henderson, one of the two men convicted of murdering twenty-one-year-old gay man Matthew Shepard near Laramie, Wyoming, in 1998, was motivated, consciously or unconsciously, by the doctrine of blood atonement.

52 Mormons Mitt Romney and Jon Huntsman will almost certainly seek the nomination of the Republican Party for president in 2012 or 2016.

III   The Folly of Populist Piety

1 See, for example, Matthew 18:3–4; Mark 10:14–15; 1 Corinthians 1:18–21, 25; and 1 Corinthians 3:18–19.

2 For more on the counter-Enlightenment tradition that treats ignorance as a virtue, see Mark Lilla, "Ignorance and Bliss," *Wilson Quarterly* 25, no. 3 (Summer 2001).

3 In a footnote to his classic study, *Anti-Intellectualism in American Life* (New York: Vintage Books, 1963), 48–49, n. 8, Richard Hofstadter reconstructs the process whereby an evangelical concludes that ignorance is preferable to intelligence: "One begins with the hardly contestable proposition that religious faith is not, in the main, propagated by logic or learning. One moves on from this to the idea that it is best propagated (in the judgment of Christ and on historical evidence) by men who have been unlearned and ignorant. It seems to follow from this that the kind of wisdom and truth possessed by such men is superior to what learned and cultivated minds have. In fact, learning and cultivation appear to be handicaps in the propagation of faith. And since the propagation of faith is the most important task before man, those who are 'ignorant as babes'

have, in the most fundamental virtue, greater strength than men who have addicted themselves to logic and learning. Accordingly, though one shrinks from a bold statement of the conclusion, humble ignorance is far better as a human quality than a cultivated mind. At bottom, this proposition, despite all the difficulties that attend it, has been eminently congenial to both evangelicalism and to American democracy."

4 On the rise of democracy in the decades separating the Revolution and the Civil War, see Sean Wilentz, *The Rise of American Democracy: Jefferson to Lincoln* (New York: W. W. Norton, 2005). Thomas Paine's *Common Sense*, published in early 1776, went through twenty-five editions in its first year of publication, selling roughly 500,000 copies at a time when the population of the American colonies was approximately 2.5 million.

5 Mark A. Noll, *The Scandal of the Evangelical Mind* (Grand Rapids, MI: Eerdmans, 1994), 60–61. On the Great Awakening more generally, see Mark A. Noll, *A History of Christianity in the United States and Canada* (Grand Rapids, MI: Eerdmans, 1992), 91ff.

6 Nathan O. Hatch, *The Democratization of American Christianity* (New Haven: Yale University Press, 1989), 5.

7 Ibid., 9–10, 7. "Beyond any doubts or fears or thoughts of being . . . deceived" is a 1775 quotation from Henry Alline, who renounced the stern Calvinism of his youth in favor of a more enthusiastic form of religious experience. See also p. 216, where Hatch notes that to this day many Americans in the heartland retain "an abiding conviction that preachers, above all, should be persons blessed with the common touch rather than oracles of high culture."

8 Ibid., 212.

9 Ibid., 7.

10 Ibid., 9.

11 With its historical roots in Scotland, the Presbyterian Church was the primary path for the Common Sense philosophy into the United States. It found an institutional home at Princeton Theological Seminary.

12 George M. Marsden, *Fundamentalism and American Culture*, 2nd ed. (New York: Oxford University Press, 2006), 110–11. See also 55–62 and Mark A. Noll, "Common Sense Traditions and American Evangelical Thought," *American Quarterly* 37 (Summer 1985).

13 Marsden, *Fundamentalism*, 116.

14 Interestingly, though unsurprisingly, partisans of the North and South in the Civil War each appealed to common sense against the other.

15 Marsden, *Fundamentalism*, 114.

16 Noll, *Scandal*, 66; Marsden, *Fundamentalism*, 6.

17 Noll, *Scandal*, 117–19. For a fuller account of radical apocalyptic speculation, see Paul Boyer, *When Time Shall Be No More: Prophecy Belief in Modern American Culture* (Cambridge, MA: Harvard University Press, 1991).

18 Charles Hodge quoted in Marsden, *Fundamentalism*, 113.

19 Ibid., 113.

20 Noll, *Scandal*, 116.

21 Tomlinson quoted in Hatch, *Democratization*, 215.

22 Historian Grant Wacker quoted in ibid., 216. See also Grant Wacker, *Heaven Below: Early Pentecostalism and American Culture* (Cambridge, MA: Harvard University Press, 2001).

23 Theological modernism was strongest in the Congregationalist and (Northern) Baptist denominations.

24 Noll, *Scandal*, 14.

25 Canadian scholar N. K. Clifford quoted in ibid., 12–13.

26 Ibid., 127.

27 Ibid., 137.

28 Marsden, *Fundamentalism*, 118.

29 Ibid., 175.

30 Ibid., 121.

31 Ibid., 141.

32 Butler Act quoted in Jerry Coyne, "The Faith That Dare Not Speak Its Name," *New Republic*, August 22 and 29, 2005, 22.

33 William Jennings Bryan quoted in Marsden, *Fundamentalism*, 213.

34 There is a voluminous literature on the conflict between religion and Darwinian evolution. See, for example, Jon H. Roberts, *Darwinism and the Divine in America: Protestant Intellectuals and Organic Evolution, 1859–1900* (Madison, WI: University of Wisconsin Press, 1988); James R. Moore, *The Post-Darwinian Controversies: A Study of the Protestant Struggle to Come to Terms with Darwinism in Great Britain and America, 1870–1900* (Cambridge: Cambridge University Press, 1979); David N. Livingstone, *Darwin's Forgotten Defenders: The Encounter Between Evangelical Theology and Evolutionary Thought* (Grand Rapids, MI: Eerdmans, 1987); John C. Greene, *Darwin and the Modern World View* (Baton Rouge: Louisiana State University Press, 1961).

35 Noll, *Scandal*, 189. See also Ronald Numbers, *The Creationists: The Evolution of Scientific Creationism* (New York: Knopf, 1992).

36 Noll, *Scandal*, 190–92.

37 In more recent years, popular referenda in such states as Kansas and Texas have prevented or turned back efforts to teach creationism in public schools.

38 Sticker quoted in Coyne, "Faith," 22.

39 Ibid., 23.

40 William Dembski quoted in ibid., 32.

41 See, for example, Phillip E. Johnson, *Darwin on Trial* (Westmont, IL: Intervarsity Press, 1993); Phillip E. Johnson, "Evolution as Dogma: The Establishment of Naturalism," *First Things*, October 1990; Phillip E. Johnson, "Creator or Blind Watchmaker?" *First Things*, January 1993.

42 Coyne, "Faith," 27.

43 Ibid., 28.

44 Michael Behe, *Darwin's Black Box: The Biochemical Challenge to Evolution* (New York: Free Press, 1998).

45 Coyne, "Faith," 31.

46 Literary critic Lionel Trilling famously described liberalism at its best as open to "variousness, possibility, complexity, and difficulty." See "Preface to *The Liberal Imagination*" in *The Moral Obligation to Be Intelligent*, ed. Leon Wieseltier (New York: Farrar, Straus and Giroux, 2000), 548.

47 Alan Wolfe, "The Opening of the Evangelical Mind," *Atlantic Monthly*, October 2000.

48 Mark A. Noll, "The Evangelical Mind Today," *First Things*, October 2004.

IV   The Perils of Providential Thinking

1 Exactly how many Americans today think in providential terms about the country is unclear. A 2006 Harris poll, for example, lists 29 percent of respondents believing that "God controls what happens on earth." Aside from the fact that this Internet-based survey was self-selecting and thus inapplicable to the general population, the wording of the question implies a very strong notion of providence—one in which God controls everything that happens, including the behavior of human beings, who are reduced to the status of marionettes in the hands of the divine. A more carefully and cautiously worded question—like, for instance, "Do you believe that God plays a role in guiding America's actions in the world?"—would almost certainly have yielded a higher affirmative response. See http://www.harrisinteractive.com/harris_poll/index.asp? PID=707.

2 Abraham Lincoln, speech to the New Jersey Senate, February 21, 1861: "I shall be most happy indeed if I shall be an humble instrument in the hands of the Almighty, and of this, his almost chosen people."

3 Quoted in Stephen H. Webb, *American Providence: A Nation with a Mission* (New York: Continuum, 2004), 90. The discussion in this and the following paragraph is indebted to Webb's narrative of the Puritan exodus on pages 31–33.

4 The phrase is historian Perry Miller's. See also Anders Stephanson, *Manifest Destiny: American Expansion and the Empire of Right* (New York: Hill and Wang, 1995), 5: "The world as God's 'manifestation' and history as predetermined 'destiny' had been ideological staples of the strongly providentialist period in England between 1620 and 1660, during which, of course, the initial migration to New England took place."

5 Quoted in Russel B. Nye, *This Almost Chosen People: Essays in the History of American Ideas* (East Lansing: Michigan State University Press, 1966), 192.

6 Edward Johnson, *Wonderworking Providence of Zion's Savior, 1628–1651*, ed. J. Franklin Jameson, Ph.D., LL.D. (New York: Charles Scribner's Sons, 1910; originally published 1654), 25.

7 Minister Thomas Thacher of Boston's Old South Church concurred with the judgment, boldly asserting that "we are the people that do succeed Israel." Clergyman and historian Thomas Prince nicely summed up the theological consensus on the topic when he observed in 1730 that "there never was any people on earth so parallel in their general history to that of the ancient Israelites as this of New England." All quotes in John F. Berens, *Providence and Patriotism in Early America, 1640–1815* (Charlottesville: University Press of Virginia, 1978), 17–19.

8 Johnson quoted in Nye, *This Almost Chosen People*, 172.

9 The phrase "new Israel" is Webb's, in *American Providence*, 33. Based on an argument of Berens, in *Providence and Patriotism*, 3, 14.

10 Berens, *Providence and Patriotism*, 3.

11 James Wilson quoted in Nye, *This Almost Chosen People*, 173.

12 Eschatological thinking in America has tended to take the form of "postmillennialism," i.e., the view that Christ's return and final judgment will follow the millennium. But there are prominent exceptions, including the Mormons, whose unique form of premillennialism (i.e., the view that Christ will reign on earth for a thousand years prior to his final judgment) we will examine below.

13 Manifest destiny was hardly new. It was, on the contrary, merely the application of very old American theological convictions to the dramatically changed national and religious circumstances of the mid-nineteenth century. Or, as Richard T. Hughes writes in *Myths Americans Live By* (Champaign: University of Illinois Press, 2003), 106, the concept of manifest destiny "was writ large on the hearts and minds of the American people long before the term itself appeared in print."

14 Quoted in Hughes, *Myths*, 106.

15 Quoted in Nye, *This Almost Chosen People*, 188.

16 Quoted in Ernest Lee Tuveson, *Redeemer Nation: The Idea of America's Millen-nial Role* (Chicago: University of Chicago Press, 1968), vii.

17 Quoted in Nye, *This Almost Chosen People*, 176–77. See also Hofstadter, *Anti-Intellectualism in American Life*, 3–5, 221–27.

18 See, in particular, Bush's second inaugural address.

19 For a thorough account of this nearly forgotten chapter of our national history, see Philip Hamburger, *Separation of Church and State* (Cambridge, MA: Harvard University Press, 2002).

20 They were also far more egalitarian. See Hatch, *Democratization*.

21 For a rare institutional expression of fidelity to the Calvinist providential narrative by the American Catholic Church, see the statement of the Third Plenary Council of Baltimore in 1884, where the church declared, "We consider the establishment of our country's independence, the shaping of its liberties and laws, as the work of special providence, its framers 'building better than they knew,' the Almighty's hand guiding them."

22 For more on how Catholicism's distinctive view of freedom contributed to its alienation from American life, see McGreevy, *Catholicism*, 36–37.

23 Much has been written on the American "Catholic moment" of the 1950s—a moment that culminated in the election of the nation's first Catholic president in 1960. For a compelling biographical account of four writers who helped bring Catholicism into the American mainstream during these years (Flannery O'Connor, Walker Percy, Thomas Merton, and Dorothy Day), see Paul Elie, *The Life You Save May Be Your Own: An American Pilgrimage* (New York: Farrar, Straus, and Giroux, 2003).

24 Patrick Allitt, *Catholic Intellectuals and Conservative Politics in America, 1950–1985* (Ithaca, NY: Cornell University Press, 1993), 34.

25 Murray, *We Hold These Truths*, 41.

26 Ibid., 30.

27 Ibid., 32.

28 Ibid., 33–34.

29 Ibid., 35–36. This blatantly illiberal definition of freedom comes from Lord Acton, whom Murray quotes as defining freedom as "not the power of doing what we like, but the right of being able to do what we ought."

30 Ibid., 36–39.

31 See Linker, *Theocons*.

32 Murray, *We Hold These Truths*, 43.

33 Neuhaus, in particular, worried about the "striking scarcity of thinking about America theologically" and urged devout American Christians "to think again—to think deeply, to think theologically—about the story of America

and its place in the story of the world." See his essay "Our American Babylon," *First Things*, December 2005, and the book *American Babylon: Notes of a Christian Exile* (New York: Basic Books, 2009). In the 2005 essay, Neuhaus also recommends Murray's model of Catholic cultural engagement as the best hope for reviving providential thinking in our time: "In the vision of John Courtney Murray, public discourse guided by appeal to natural law—and accompanied by the presence of a Church that effectively challenged democracy's idolatrous aspirations to ultimacy—could provide a public philosophy for sustaining the American experiment in producing as just and free a society as possible. . . ."

34 Scholars Gustav H. Blanke and Karen Lynn quoted in Jeffrey C. Fox, *Latter-Day Political Views* (Lanham, MD: Rowman and Littlefield, 2006), 43.

35 1 Nephi 13:12–20, quoted in Fox, *Latter-Day Political Views*, 42.

36 2 Nephi 10:11–14.

37 3 Nephi 21:4.

38 Ether 2:12.

39 Fox, *Latter-Day Political Views*, 42, quotes prominent church leader Ezra Taft Benson as saying, "Yes, the Lord planned it all. Why? So America could serve as a beacon of liberty and in preparation for the opening of a new gospel dispensation—the last and greatest of all dispensations in preparation for the second coming of the Lord Jesus Christ."

40 Quoted in Bushman, *Joseph Smith*, 519. Joseph Smith's successor prophet, Brigham Young, upheld this prophecy, declaring during a sermon on December 23, 1866, that at Christ's second coming he would return to "the land of America." Cited in Abanes, *One Nation*, 479, n. 15.

41 In the years leading up to Smith's June 1844 assassination, the Mormons were frequent victims of deadly mob violence, most of it motivated by fear of their unusual beliefs and practices as well as anger at their opposition to slavery and tendency to vote as a block wherever they settled. Missouri governor Lillburn W. Boggs arguably incited the worst of this violence by declaring that "the Mormons must be treated as enemies, and must be exterminated or driven from the state, if necessary, for the public good." (Boggs quoted in Fox, *Latter-Day Political Views*, 27.)

42 Abanes, *One Nation*, 186, and Bushman, *Joseph Smith*, 522.

43 Abanes, *One Nation*, 188.

44 Bushman, *Joseph Smith*, 520–21. See also Abanes, *One Nation*, 187, who quotes Smith confidant Wilford Woodruff saying that the council's stated purpose was to "organize the political Kingdom of God in preparation for the second coming of Christ."

45 Smith quoted in Abanes, *One Nation*, 185. Wight quoted in Bushman, *Joseph Smith*, 521.

46 Smith quoted in Abanes, *One Nation*, xvii.

47 See ibid., 478–79, n. 1 for this list as well as a thorough discussion of the controversy surrounding the prophecy. See also pp. 434–36 for a collection of quotations from prominent twentieth-century Mormons affirming the LDS belief that a Mormon and/or the Mormon church will one day save the Constitution and nation.

48 Senator Orrin Hatch on *The Doug Wright Show*, KSL, November 9, 1999. See also John Heilprin, "Did Hatch Allude to LDS Prophecy?" *Salt Lake Tribune*, November 11, 1999, and the discussion in Abanes, *One Nation*, xvii ff.

49 I know of no evidence that Mitt Romney made similar prophetic allusions in his public statements during his run for the White House in 2007–2008.

50 Isaiah Berlin, "Historical Inevitability," in *The Proper Study of Mankind: An Anthology of Essays* (New York: Farrar, Straus, and Giroux, 1998), 129–30.

51 Ibid., 131–32.

52 Ibid., 189.

53 Berlin's essay was written under the influence of Karl Popper's philosophy of science, which defines empirical knowledge as a theory or hypothesis that is in principle disprovable, or "falsifiable," by further observation or experiment.

54 Berlin, "Historical Inevitability," 130–32, 185.

55 Augustine, *City of God*, trans. Henry Bettenson (New York: Penguin Classics, 2003), 196.

56 Ibid., 216.

57 Ibid., 143.

58 Alexis de Tocqueville, *Democracy in America*, Vol. I, Ch. 15. This famous quotation comes from the Henry Reeve translation, revised and corrected in 1899, which is available online at several locations.

59 Niebuhr's main rival for the title of leading twentieth-century Augustinian would be the Swiss theologian Karl Barth. Barth was undeniably the greater theologian, though he was also arguably further removed in spirit from Augustine than Niebuhr.

60 Reinhold Niebuhr, *The Irony of American History* (New York: Charles Scribner's Sons, 1952), 28.

61 Ibid., 42.

62 Ibid., 88.

63 Ibid., 133.

64 Ibid., 134.

65 Ibid., 151, 140. See also p. 145 for America's need for "heroic patience." For a discussion of the difficulty of judging in one's own case, see Aristotle, *Politics*, Book III, Ch. 9.

66 Niebuhr, *Irony*, 173.

67 Niebuhr quoted in Langdon Gilkey, *On Niebuhr: A Theological Study* (Chicago: University of Chicago Press, 2001), 211.

68 For Niebuhr's interpretation of the second inaugural address, see 171–72.

69 See, for example, Obama's remarks in Cairo, Egypt, on June 4, 2009, http://www.whitehouse.gov/the_press_office/Remarks-by-the-President-at-Cairo-University-6-04-09/.

V   The Impossibility of Sexual Consensus

1 The members of this (informal) coalition include Focus on the Family, Family Research Council, World Congress of Families, Christian Broadcasting Network, Christian Coalition, Eagle Forum, Trinity Broadcasting Network, American Life League, National Right to Life, Americans United for Life Action, American Center for Law and Justice, and Concerned Women for America.

2 See, for example, Linker, *Theocons*, Ch. 7, and Andrew Sullivan, *The Conservative Soul: Fundamentalism, Freedom, and the Future of the Right* (New York: Harper Perennial, 2007), Chs. 2 and 3, where the author examines the fundamentalist Christian outlook on the world, which he dubs "Christianism."

3 This is of course a quotation from and reference to Lincoln's "House Divided" speech, delivered on June 16, 1858. The same universalizing dynamic has been at work with regard to abortion ever since the *Roe v. Wade* decision of 1973.

4 See Alasdair MacIntyre, *After Virtue: A Study in Moral Theory*, 3rd ed. (Notre Dame, IN: University of Notre Dame Press, 2007) and Richard John Neuhaus, *The Naked Public Square: Religion and Democracy in America*, 2nd ed. (Grand Rapids, MI: Eerdmans, 1986).

5 By "liberal political tradition," I mean the tradition that advocates the form of government (the political principles and institutions) that prevails in the United States, western Europe, and in parts of Asia and Latin America, not the political faction associated with the Democratic Party in the United States, which also goes by the name of "liberal." Despite their hostility to the liberalism of the Democratic Party, nearly all members of the Republican Party are liberals in the more expansive sense of the term I employ throughout this book. For more on this terminological distinction, see the Introduction above.

6 See, for example, Robert P. George, *The Clash of Orthodoxies: Law, Religion, and Morality in Crisis* (Wilmington, DE: ISI Books, 2001).

7   How many challenges are enough to trigger the retreat of the liberal state
    from enforcing illiberal laws? It differs from case to case. When it came to
    race, a fairly large number were required because blacks had virtually no politi-
    cal voice at all. Fewer have been needed on issues related to sex because sex
    touches everyone. Euthanasia—the most significant nonsexual issue wrapped
    up with the culture war—may very well be the next issue to reach a tipping
    point after same-sex marriage is settled. Because there is no nonreligious argu-
    ment in favor of banning (legally) the taking of one's own life, the outcome of
    the dispute over euthanasia is close to certain: it will one day be decriminalized
    throughout the country.

8   On marriage as a "one-flesh" union, see George, *Clash of Orthodoxies*, 77ff.

9   It is striking how often talk among sexual traditionalists about same-sex mar-
    riage devolves into a conversation about bestiality.

10 As historian George Chauncey points out, the Catholic Welfare Committee
    (CWC) strenuously opposed the very modest liberalization of marriage law
    in 1934 to allow divorce on the grounds of desertion, a reform that permitted
    women to remarry after having been abandoned by their husbands. Allowing
    such a change in marriage law would, the CWC argued, "weaken the law con-
    cerning . . . marital status" and thus "strike at the foundation of society," since
    marriage is the basis of the family—and the family is the cornerstone of soci-
    ety." See George Chauncey, *Why Marriage? The History Shaping Today's Debate
    over Gay Equality* (New York: Basic Books, 2004), 83–84.

11 See, for example, Bruce Bagemihl, *Biological Exuberance: Animal Homosexual-
    ity and Natural Diversity* (New York: St. Martin's Press, 1999); Volker Sommer
    and Paul L. Vasey, *Homosexual Behaviour in Animals: An Evolutionary Perspec-
    tive* (Cambridge: Cambridge University Press, 2006); and Nathan W. Bailey and
    Marlene Zuk, "Same-Sex Sexual Behavior and Evolution," *Trends in Ecology &
    Evolution* 24, no. 8 (June 2009).

12 See Andrew Sullivan, *Virtually Normal: An Argument About Homosexual-
    ity* (New York: Vintage Books, 1996); Jonathan Rauch, *Gay Marriage: Why It
    Is Good for Gays, Good for Straights, and Good for America* (New York: Times
    Books, 2004); and Evan Wolfson, *Why Marriage Matters: America, Equality, and
    Gay People's Right to Marry* (New York: Simon and Schuster, 2005).

13 See Leon Kass, "The Wisdom of Repugnance," *New Republic*, June 2, 1997,
    17–26.

14 Aside from his general moral traditionalism, I have no reason to suspect that
    Kass himself would endorse such a claim. I am merely applying the logic of his
    argument against cloning to the issue of homosexuality.

15 Many of those who take this position have been influenced by the antimodern-ist writings of Catholic philosopher Alasdair MacIntyre, agrarian poet Wendell Berry, and sociologist Christopher Lasch. Two of the most impressive and tire-less spokesmen for this view are the Georgetown University political theorist Patrick Deneen and the journalist Rod Dreher. See also the other writers affili-ated with the website Front Porch Republic, http://www.frontporchrepublic .com/.

16 See Nate Silver's analysis showing when gay marriage is likely to be accepted in the various states, http://www.fivethirtyeight.com/2009/04/will-iowans-uphold-gay-marriage.html.

17 For a useful introduction to the legal issues involved in these various scenarios, see the helpful discussion at http://pewforum.org/events/?EventID=216.

18 For more on liberalism's role in motivating the Christian home-schooling movement, see the discussion in Chapter 1, above.

19 Indeed, I used to be one of those writers.

20 In an important 2006 article analyzing the likely consequences of overturn-ing *Roe*, legal affairs journalist Jeffrey Rosen predicted that a woman's right to choose would be secure in twenty-three states, while as many as a dozen might have draconian restrictions in place. That would leave fifteen states somewhere in the middle—probably allowing abortion in the first trimester and then regu-lating it rather quickly after that, with probable exceptions for the health of the mother. This middle position quite accurately captures the position of the American people. As Rosen notes, over the past thirty years, polls have consis-tently shown that two-thirds of Americans think abortion should be legal in the first trimester, with support falling to 25 percent in the second trimester, and only 10 percent supporting its legality in the third trimester. Events in the years since Rosen's article give us reason to think he may have been too pessimistic. In March 2006, South Dakota's legislature passed a law banning all abortions except when a woman's life is seriously threatened, convincing some that this was a glimpse of a post-*Roe* America. But in fact the law provoked a significant backlash in the state, leading to the repeal of the law through a referendum on election day 2008. See Rosen, "The Day After *Roe*," *Atlantic*, June 2006.

21 I'd like to thank Ed Kilgore for persuading me that this is the more likely out-come of a reversal of *Roe*.

22 Then there are those situations marked by a different and more intense form of tragedy—when the pregnancy is wanted but modern medical technology reveals that the fetus suffers from a debilitating defect. For more on these increasingly common circumstances, see below.

23 Byard Duncan, "My First Abortion Party," *AlterNet*, July 8, 2009, http://www
.alternet.org/reproductivejustice/141140/my_first_abortion_party/.

24 A number of the polls collected at PollingReport.com (http://www.polling
report.com/abortion.htm) show that people's attitudes toward abortion change
drastically depending on the reasons given for undertaking the procedure. See,
especially, the Fox News/Opinion Dynamics poll of October 23–24, 2007, and
the CNN/USA Today/Gallup poll of January 10–12, 2003.

25 See, for example, Patrick Lee and Robert P. George, "The Wrong of Abortion,"
in Andrew I. Cohen and Christopher Wellman, eds., *Contemporary Debates in
Applied Ethics* (New York: Blackwell Publishers, 2005), 14.

26 As journalist and bioethicist William Saletan has noted, there is little evidence that simply making birth control more widely available will lower rates
of unwanted pregnancies. The state must go further, to actively advocate its
use. See Saletan, "This Is the Way the Culture Wars End," *New York Times*,
February 21, 2009: "Eight years ago, the Alan Guttmacher Institute surveyed
over 10,000 American women who had abortions. Nearly half said they hadn't
used birth control in the month they conceived. When asked why not, 8 percent
cited financial problems, and 2 percent said they didn't know where to get it. By
comparison, 28 percent said they had thought they wouldn't get pregnant, 26
percent said they hadn't expected to have sex and 23 percent said they had never
thought about using birth control, had never gotten around to it or had stopped
using it. Ten percent said their partners had objected to it. Three percent said
they had thought it would make sex less fun. This isn't a shortage of pills or
condoms. It's a shortage of cultural and personal responsibility. It's a failure to
teach, understand, admit or care that unprotected sex can lead to the creation—
and the subsequent killing, through abortion—of a developing human being."
See also the illuminating followup discussion in *Slate*, where Saletan responds
to the skepticism of pro-life Catholic conservative Ross Douthat: http://www
.slate.com/blogs/blogs/humannature/archive/2009/02/27/selling-rubbers
.aspx.

27 This figure is extremely consistent, showing up in a number of the polls collected at http://www.pollingreport.com/abortion.htm.

VI   The Intolerance of the Freethinkers

1 Richard Dawkins, *The God Delusion* (Boston: Houghton Mifflin, 2006), 317–18.
2 Mytton quoted in ibid., 325.
3 Humphrey quoted in ibid., 326.

4   Sam Harris, *The End of Faith* (New York: W. W. Norton, 2004), 23. The second bestseller is the more narrowly focused *Letter to a Christian Nation* (New York: Knopf, 2007).

5   Christopher Hitchens, *God Is Not Great: How Religion Poisons Everything* (New York: Twelve Books, 2007), 283.

6   For more on French atheism in the early modern period, see Alan Kors, *Atheism in France, 1650–1729* (Princeton, NJ: Princeton University Press, 1990).

7   A selection of Hébert's pamphlets in rough English translations can be found on a Marxist website: http://www.marxists.org/glossary/people/h/e.htm#hebert-jacques.

8   Karl Marx, "On the Jewish Question," in *The Marx–Engels Reader*, ed. Robert C. Tucker (New York: W. W. Norton, 1978), 30.

9   Ibid., 29.

10 Ibid., 35.

11 Ibid., 32.

12 Ibid., 46.

13 Ibid., 48.

14 Ibid., 52.

15 See Jeffrey Herf, *Reactionary Modernism: Technology, Culture, and Politics, in Weimar and the Third Reich* (Cambridge: Cambridge University Press, 1984).

16 Sidney Hook, "Religion and the Intellectuals," in *The Quest for Being* (Amherst, NY: Prometheus Books, 1991), 100.

17 For more on these and many other "freethinkers" in American history, see Susan Jacoby, *Freethinkers: A History of American Secularism* (New York: Metropolitan Books, 2004).

18 The interview is available online at http://www.positiveatheism.org/hist/mad play.htm.

19 Dawkins does attempt to fashion an original argument against God at one point in *The God Delusion*, asserting that entities (like the biblical God) who are capable of creativity only arise at the end of a complex evolutionary process, not at its beginning. While an interesting claim, it accomplishes very little against a believer, since, like the circular arguments of Daniel Dennett in *Breaking the Spell: Religion as a Natural Phenomenon* (New York: Viking, 2006), it assumes something an intelligent believer would deny—namely, that Darwinian evolution can account for the origins of all forms of intelligence.

20 Hitchens, *God Is Not Great*, 12–13, 107, 113.

21 Harris, *End of Faith*, 15.

22 Ibid., 323.

23 Ibid., 20–21.

24 Dawkins agrees with, and adds to, Harris's assault on religious moderation. See *The God Delusion*, 306–8.

25 Harris, *Letter to a Christian Nation*, 91.

26 For more on liberalism's attempt to decouple politics from theology, see Mark Lilla, *The Stillborn God: Religion, Politics, and the Modern West* (New York: Knopf, 2007), Ch. 2.

27 Plato, *Apology of Socrates*, line 21d.

28 Ibid., lines 29dff and 36a–38b.

29 David Hume, *The Natural History of Religion* in *Writings on Religion* (Chicago: Open Court Books, 1992; originally published 1757), 182.

30 The term "peace of mind" (*ataraxia*) derives from the writings of Sextus Empiricus.

31 The fullest surviving statement of Epicureanism can be found in Lucretius, *On the Nature of Things*, trans. Walter Englert (Newburyport, MA: Focus Publishing, 2003).

32 Voltaire's poem on the Lisbon earthquake can be found online at http://en.wikisource.org/wiki/Poem_on_the_Lisbon_Disaster.

33 The phrase "tragic stoicism" comes from James Wood, "The Sickness unto Life," *New Republic*, November 8, 1999.

34 Albert Camus, *The Myth of Sisyphus and Other Essays* (New York: Vintage International, 1991), 28.

35 Ibid., 123.

36 Philip Larkin, "Aubade," in *Collected Poems* (New York: Farrar, Straus, and Giroux, 2003), 190–91.

37 Larkin, "Church Going," in ibid., 58–59.

38 Larkin, "Faith Healing," in ibid., 86.

39 Friedrich Nietzsche, *The Will to Power*, trans. Walter Kaufmann (New York: Vintage Books, 1968), Aphorism 435.

40 Nietzsche introduced the idea of the death of God in *The Gay Science*, trans. Walter Kaufmann (New York: Vintage Books, 1974), Aphorism 125, and he returned to it in *Thus Spoke Zarathustra*, trans. Walter Kaufmann (New York: The Modern Library, 1995), 10–12.

41 Nietzsche, *Zarathustra*, 16–19.

42 The phrase "the abolition of man" comes from Christian apologist C. S. Lewis, whose concerns in this matter were quite similar to Nietzsche's.

43 Nietzsche, *The Genealogy of Morals*, in *The Basic Writings of Nietzsche*, trans. Walter Kaufmann (New York: The Modern Library, 1992), Essay III, Aphorism 27.

44 Among the many works that explore the Nietzschean theme of the relationship between truth and illusion on the one hand with human happiness and flourishing on the other are Eugene O'Neill's *The Iceman Cometh*, Samuel Beckett's *Waiting for Godot* and *Endgame*, and Emil Cioran's oeuvre as a whole.

45 http://scienceblogs.com/pharyngula/2008/07/its_a_goddamned_cracker.php.

46 http://scienceblogs.com/pharyngula/2008/07/the_great_desecration.php.

47 http://www.gc.cuny.edu/faculty/research_briefs/aris/aris_index.htm.

48 Or in the words of political philosopher Leo Strauss, "Every one of us can be and ought to be . . . [a] philosopher open to the challenge of theology, or [a] theologian open to the challenge of philosophy." See "Progress or Return?" in *Jewish Philosophy and the Crisis of Modernity: Essays and Lectures in Modern Jewish Thought*, ed. with an introduction by Kenneth Hart Green (Albany: State University of New York Press, 1997), 116.

Epilogue: Religion in a Centerless Society

1 The rise of pluralism in Europe had other causes besides the Reformation and its aftermath. The collapse of the feudal order and subsequent rise of a commercial middle class introduced the first signs of the social dynamism we associate with capitalism. Scientific discoveries inspired skepticism about the Aristotelianism that had unified the elite mind of Europe for hundreds of years. And then there was the immense size of nation-states, which made them much more potentially diverse and cosmopolitan than the ancient city-states that gave birth to the ideal of political unity.

2 The idea of the centerless society comes from the work of German sociologist Niklas Luhmann. For the best introduction to his thought and its implications for liberal politics, as well as for a simpler version of the "mailman" example elaborated above, see the introductory essay by Stephen Holmes and Charles Larmore in their collection of Luhmann's writings, *The Differentiation of Society* (New York: Columbia University Press, 1982).

3 For more on the "liberal bargain," see Linker, *Theocons*, 224–7.

4 The following argument adapts certain insights from Aristotle's *Politics* (Book III), where the ancient philosopher examines the question of whether and under what circumstances a good citizen can be a good human being in general (meaning someone who reaches the peak of human excellence). His answer was that it depends on the character of the political community in which one is a citizen. In the worst political communities—in Nazi Germany or the Soviet Union, for example—it may very well be impossible for a good citizen to be a

good human being, or for a good human being to be a good citizen, because citizenship in those communities requires behavior diametrically opposed to human excellence. In more decent political communities, by contrast, much more overlap will be possible; in most cases, a good citizen will be quite capable of being a good human being, and vice versa. Yet the overlap will never be total—because, for Aristotle, human excellence at its peak involves disinterested philosophical contemplation of the eternal truth, while politics at its peak (statesmanship) demands active devotion to the common good of a particular political community. Aristotle indicated that only in an imaginary best political community would political excellence harmonize perfectly with human excellence in general. In the real world of imperfect political communities, the two ideals will always diverge because they serve different ends. In the following paragraphs I argue that a similar dynamic can be seen at play in the relationship between traditionalist religion and liberal politics.

5 See Christian Smith, *Soul Searching: The Religious and Spiritual Lives of American Teenagers* (New York: Oxford University Press, 2005) and *Souls in Transition: The Religious and Spiritual Lives of Emerging Adults* (New York: Oxford University Press, 2009). See also Alan Wolfe, *Moral Freedom: The Search for Virtue in a World of Choice* (New York: W. W. Norton, 2001).

Index

Roman Empire, 133
Romney, Mitt, 221*n*, 228*n*
Roosevelt, Franklin Delano, 69
Root, Erik, 49
Rosen, Jeffrey, 231*n*
Rosin, Hanna, 49
Rousseau, Jean-Jacques, 182
Rumspringa, 23–24
Rushdoony, Rousas John, 41–42, 43
Ryan, John A., 69

Sagan, Carl, 173
Salafism, 34, 36, 39
Saletan, William, 232*n*
same-sex marriage, 141–42, 147–58, 160,
    230*n*
  fear of change and, 152–54
  morality of rights in, 155
  paleoconservative arguments against,
    154–55
  religious freedom and, 157–58
  social consequences of, 152–54
  "wisdom of repugnance" argument
    against, 151–52
Sanger, Margaret, 177
Schachter, Rabbi Herschel, 212*n*
Schaeffer, Francis A., 41
Schlafly, Phyllis, 44
science, 93, 99–100, 107, 109
  Amish and, 23
  Popper's philosophy of, 228*n*
  theory in, 103–4
  two forms of, 102
scientific method, 19, 53
Scopes, John, 100
Scopes "Monkey" Trial, 100–101
secular humanism, 41, 46, 54
self-evidence, political, 88–90
Senate, U.S., 73, 120

separation of church and state, 66, 68,
    203
separatism, 202
  of Amish, 21
  of Christian Reconstructionism, 41–42
  of evangelicals, 45
  of Haredi Jews, 31
  of home-schooling movement, 44–45,
    50, 51
  of Islam, 36
  liberalism and, 26
  of Orthodox Jews, 212*n*
September 11, 2001, terrorist attacks of,
    37, 61, 113, 179
Seventh-Day Adventists, 44, 77, 87, 101,
    119
sexual morality, 53, 139–68, 202
sexual revolution, 148
sexual traditionalism, 155, 165
  consensus on, 146–47
  of Haredi Jews, 29
  and same-sex marriage, 147–58
Shakers, 77
Sharia, 33, 36, 39
Sheldon, Charles, 97
Shepard, Matthew, 221*n*
"shunning" (*Meidung*), 24, 211*n*
sin, 58, 86
sincerity, 59–62
Sisyphus, 188
skepticism, 132, 172, 174, 183, 184–85,
    191, 192
slavery, 14, 137, 142, 150, 156
Smith, Christian, 204
Smith, Joseph, 77, 78, 79, 80, 81, 126,
    127, 128, 129, 227*n*
  presidential campaign of, 128–29
Smith, Joseph F., 129
Smith, Joseph Fielding, 80, 129